Practical Machine Learning with Python and Scikit-Learn

Engineer High-Impact Machine Learning Models with Pythonic Precision and Scikit-Learn Mastery

THOMPSON CARTER

Table of Contents

Chapter 1

Introduction to Machine Learning and Scikit-Learn

Machine learning has emerged as one of the most impactful technologies in the modern data-driven world. It allows systems to automatically learn from data, improve from experience, and make predictions or decisions without being explicitly programmed. In this chapter, we will explore the core principles of machine learning, delve into its fundamental concepts, and understand the pivotal role Scikit-Learn plays in Python-based development. This foundation is crucial for grasping the relationship between machine learning algorithms, data, and Scikit-Learn's versatile utilities.

What is Machine Learning?

Machine learning is a subset of artificial intelligence (AI) that focuses on the development of algorithms that enable computers to learn and improve from data. At its core, machine learning is about creating models that can identify patterns, make predictions, and solve problems based on past data. Unlike traditional programming, where explicit instructions are provided, machine learning models extract information from large datasets and adjust themselves to improve accuracy over time.

There are three primary types of machine learning:

17

Supervised Learning

Supervised learning involves training a model on a labeled dataset, meaning the input data is paired with the correct output. The model learns to map inputs to the corresponding outputs, and after training, it can predict outcomes for new, unseen data. Common applications include classification tasks, where models are used to categorize data (e.g., spam detection in emails), and regression tasks, where models predict continuous values (e.g., housing prices).

Unsupervised Learning

In unsupervised learning, the model is trained on data without labels. The goal is to identify patterns, clusters, or associations in the data. Examples include clustering techniques like K-Means, which groups data points based on similarities, and dimensionality reduction techniques like Principal Component Analysis (PCA), which simplify complex datasets.

Reinforcement Learning

Reinforcement learning is a feedback-driven machine learning paradigm where an agent learns to make decisions by interacting with an environment. The agent is rewarded for positive actions and penalized for negative ones, and its objective is to maximize cumulative rewards. This approach is often used in robotics, game theory, and autonomous systems.

Why Python for Machine Learning?

Python has become the de facto language for machine learning and data science due to its simplicity, readability, and extensive libraries that cater to machine learning tasks. Libraries such as Numpy, Pandas, and Matplotlib make data manipulation and visualization straightforward, while more specialized libraries like TensorFlow and PyTorch focus on deep learning. However, when it comes to traditional machine learning tasks—such as classification, regression, clustering, and model evaluation—Scikit-Learn is the go-to library for Python developers.

Python's ecosystem makes it easy to integrate multiple tools and frameworks, streamlining the process of developing machine learning models. Its versatility, combined with Scikit-Learn's comprehensive set of features, enables data scientists and developers to prototype, implement, and deploy models with efficiency.

Overview of Scikit-Learn

Scikit-Learn is an open-source Python library that provides simple and efficient tools for data mining, machine learning, and data analysis. It is built on top of Python's fundamental scientific libraries, Numpy and SciPy, and offers a consistent and clean API for implementing a variety of machine learning algorithms.

Scikit-Learn is highly accessible, making it a popular choice among both beginners and experienced professionals.

Scikit-Learn simplifies the process of training, evaluating, and fine-tuning machine learning models by abstracting many of the complexities involved in these tasks. Its built-in algorithms cover a wide range of applications, from regression and classification to clustering and dimensionality reduction. Scikit-Learn also provides powerful utilities for data preprocessing, feature extraction, model selection, and hyperparameter tuning, making it an all-encompassing tool for end-to-end machine learning development.

Key Features of Scikit-Learn

Scikit-Learn's popularity stems from its flexibility, ease of use, and the wide array of tools it provides for machine learning. Some of the key features include:

1. Simple and Consistent API

Scikit-Learn offers a well-designed and consistent API across all of its machine learning algorithms. Whether you're working with regression, classification, or clustering, the process for initializing a model, fitting it to data, and making predictions follows a similar structure. This uniformity allows developers to quickly prototype different models without needing to learn new syntax for each algorithm.

2. Preprocessing and Feature Engineering

Data preprocessing is a critical step in machine learning, and Scikit-Learn provides a variety of tools for this purpose. From handling missing values to scaling, normalizing, and encoding categorical variables, Scikit-Learn makes it easy to prepare raw data for model training. Feature engineering techniques like polynomial features, feature selection, and dimensionality reduction (e.g., PCA) are also readily available.

3. Wide Range of Algorithms

Scikit-Learn implements many popular machine learning algorithms, including:

- **Linear Models**: Linear regression, logistic regression, ridge and lasso regression
- **Ensemble Methods**: Random forests, gradient boosting, and AdaBoost
- **Support Vector Machines (SVM)**
- **Nearest Neighbors**: K-nearest neighbors (KNN)
- **Clustering Algorithms**: K-means, DBSCAN, and hierarchical clustering

These algorithms can be applied across different types of machine learning tasks, giving developers the flexibility to choose the best approach for their problem.

4. Model Evaluation and Selection

Scikit-Learn provides robust tools for evaluating and selecting models, including cross-validation, performance metrics (e.g., accuracy, precision, recall), and model selection utilities like GridSearchCV and RandomizedSearchCV. These features help ensure that models generalize well to new data and are optimized for the task at hand.

5. Pipeline and Model Persistence

Scikit-Learn's pipeline feature allows developers to streamline the entire machine learning workflow by chaining together preprocessing steps and model training into a single object. This ensures that the entire process, from raw data to predictions, can be executed seamlessly. Additionally, Scikit-Learn provides utilities for saving and loading models (model persistence), which simplifies the deployment process.

Relationship Between Machine Learning Algorithms, Data, and Scikit-Learn

The interaction between machine learning algorithms, data, and Scikit-Learn is fundamental to building successful models. Machine learning algorithms are mathematical models that learn patterns from data, and their performance depends heavily on the quality and structure of that data. Scikit-Learn provides tools for both preparing the data and selecting the right algorithms, which makes it easier to train models that perform well on new, unseen data.

Data: The Foundation of Machine Learning

Data is the cornerstone of every machine learning model. The quality, quantity, and diversity of data directly impact the effectiveness of the learning process. Data may come in many forms, such as structured data (e.g., databases, spreadsheets), unstructured data (e.g., text, images), or time-series data. Scikit-Learn's utilities are designed to handle structured data, and it offers methods to transform and clean data, ensuring it is in a suitable format for model training.

Algorithms: The Learning Process

Machine learning algorithms are the engine that drives the learning process. They take input data, extract meaningful patterns, and build models that can make predictions or decisions. Different types of algorithms are suited to different tasks—linear regression is ideal for continuous prediction, while KNN or decision trees may be better suited for classification tasks. Scikit-Learn's library of algorithms allows developers to experiment with different approaches to find the best solution for their problem.

Scikit-Learn: The Glue That Binds Data and Algorithms

Scikit-Learn acts as the glue that binds data with machine learning algorithms. It provides the tools for preprocessing data, training models, and evaluating performance, all within a consistent framework. Whether you're working with regression, classification, or clustering, Scikit-Learn simplifies the entire process, enabling you to focus on refining your model rather than worrying about the details of algorithm implementation.

This introduction lays the foundation for understanding machine learning in Python and the critical role Scikit-Learn plays in this ecosystem. By providing powerful tools for data manipulation, model selection, and evaluation, Scikit-Learn empowers developers to efficiently build, test, and refine machine learning models. As we progress through this book, we will explore various machine learning concepts and algorithms in detail, all while leveraging Scikit-Learn's utilities to build practical, real-world solutions.

Chapter 2

Python for Machine Learning: Essential Concepts

Python has gained immense popularity as a go-to language for machine learning, largely because of its simplicity, flexibility, and a rich ecosystem of libraries. In this chapter, we will review the key Python features and libraries that are most relevant to machine learning, including Numpy, Pandas, and Matplotlib. Understanding these libraries and the essential concepts within them is crucial for writing efficient machine learning code. By mastering these tools, you will be able to handle data, perform complex computations, and visualize results—all of which are critical for developing robust machine learning models.

The Role of Python in Machine Learning

Python has emerged as the leading programming language for machine learning because of several advantages. Its syntax is intuitive and easy to learn, making it accessible to beginners. Python also has an extensive collection of libraries that simplify various aspects of machine learning, from data manipulation to model evaluation.

The key reasons for Python's dominance in machine learning are:

- **Ease of Use**: Python's simple and readable syntax allows developers to focus on building machine learning models without getting bogged down by complex code.
- **Rich Ecosystem of Libraries**: Python boasts a comprehensive set of libraries, such as Numpy, Pandas, Matplotlib, Scikit-Learn, TensorFlow, and PyTorch, that streamline different stages of the machine learning process.
- **Community Support**: Python has a massive community of developers and researchers who continuously contribute to open-source libraries, making it easy to find resources, tutorials, and support.

Numpy: Foundation of Numerical Computing in Python

Numpy (Numerical Python) is a fundamental library in Python, especially for handling large, multi-dimensional arrays and matrices. It is the backbone of many scientific libraries, including Scikit-Learn, and provides a powerful set of tools for numerical computations.

Numpy Arrays

The core feature of Numpy is the ndarray object, which represents an n-dimensional array of homogeneous data types. Numpy arrays are faster and more memory-efficient than Python's built-in lists, making them ideal for machine learning tasks where large datasets are involved.

For example, creating a simple Numpy array looks like this:

```
import numpy as np
arr = np.array([1, 2, 3, 4, 5])
```

This creates a one-dimensional array. You can also create multi-dimensional arrays, which are essential for representing data such as images (which are typically stored as 2D or 3D arrays) or large datasets (which can be stored in 2D arrays, or matrices).

Array Operations and Broadcasting

Numpy allows for vectorized operations, meaning you can perform element-wise operations on arrays without the need for explicit loops. This greatly improves the efficiency of computations. Additionally, Numpy supports broadcasting, a mechanism that automatically expands the dimensions of arrays to match for arithmetic operations.

For instance:

```
arr1 = np.array([1, 2, 3])
arr2 = np.array([4, 5, 6])
result = arr1 + arr2
```

Here, the addition is applied element-wise, and the result is $[5, 7, 9]$.

Linear Algebra and Random Number Generation

Machine learning often involves linear algebra operations, such as matrix multiplication, and Numpy provides efficient implementations of these operations. It also offers tools for generating random numbers, which are useful for tasks such as splitting data into training and test sets or initializing model weights.

For example, matrix multiplication can be done as follows:

```
matrix_a = np.array([[1, 2], [3, 4]])
matrix_b = np.array([[5, 6], [7, 8]])
result = np.dot(matrix_a, matrix_b)
```

Pandas: Data Manipulation and Analysis

Pandas is a powerful library for data manipulation and analysis, and it is widely used in machine learning for handling datasets. Pandas makes it easy to clean, transform, and analyze data, which is often the most time-consuming part of machine learning projects.

Series and DataFrames

The two primary data structures in Pandas are the Series and DataFrame. A Series is a one-dimensional labeled array capable of holding any data type, while a

DataFrame is a two-dimensional table with labeled axes (rows and columns). DataFrames are particularly useful for handling structured data, such as datasets in CSV or Excel files.

For example, creating a DataFrame from a dictionary:

```
import pandas as pd
data = {'Name': ['John', 'Alice', 'Bob'], 'Age': [23, 25, 30]}
df = pd.DataFrame(data)
```

This creates a table-like structure where each column has a label, and each row corresponds to a record.

Data Cleaning and Transformation

Pandas excels at handling missing data, filtering rows and columns, and transforming datasets into the required format. For example, you can fill missing values with a default value or drop rows with missing data.

```
# Drop rows with missing values
df.dropna(inplace=True)

# Fill missing values with a default value
df.fillna(0, inplace=True)
```

You can also use Pandas to filter data, apply functions to columns, or merge multiple datasets.

Handling Large Datasets

One of the strengths of Pandas is its ability to handle large datasets efficiently. Machine learning models require a lot of data, and Pandas provides functionality to read and process large files, filter irrelevant data, and join datasets from multiple sources.

For instance, reading a CSV file:

```
df = pd.read_csv('data.csv')
```

Once the data is loaded into a DataFrame, you can quickly manipulate and analyze it to gain insights or prepare it for machine learning models.

Matplotlib: Data Visualization

Data visualization is crucial in machine learning for understanding the data and interpreting the results of models. Matplotlib is a versatile Python library for creating static, animated, and interactive visualizations.

Plotting Data with Matplotlib

Matplotlib's core functionality revolves around its pyplot module, which provides a MATLAB-like interface for creating plots. Some common types of plots used in machine learning include line plots, bar charts, scatter plots, and histograms.

For example, creating a simple line plot:

```
import matplotlib.pyplot as plt
x = [1, 2, 3, 4, 5]
y = [2, 3, 5, 7, 11]
plt.plot(x, y)
plt.show()
```

This will display a basic line plot. You can customize the plot by adding labels, changing colors, and controlling the axes.

Visualizing Data Distributions

Understanding the distribution of your data is a key step in machine learning. Matplotlib can be used to create histograms, box plots, and scatter plots, which help visualize the spread, central tendency, and relationships within the data.

For example, creating a histogram:

```
plt.hist(df['Age'], bins=10)
plt.show()
```

This plot can reveal insights about the distribution of ages in your dataset, such as whether the data is skewed or has outliers.

Subplots and Customizations

Matplotlib allows for the creation of subplots, which are multiple plots within a single figure. This is useful when you want to compare different variables or visualize multiple aspects of your data side by side.

```
fig, axs = plt.subplots(2, 2)
axs[0, 0].plot(x, y)
axs[0, 1].scatter(x, y)
axs[1, 0].hist(df['Age'])
plt.show()
```

Subplots make it easier to present a comprehensive view of your data in one visual display.

Writing Efficient Machine Learning Code

In addition to mastering these libraries, writing efficient machine learning code requires a few additional best practices. Python's flexibility makes it easy to write both clean, maintainable code and highly efficient, performance-driven code.

Vectorization and Avoiding Loops

As we mentioned earlier, Numpy allows for vectorized operations, which can significantly speed up computations by eliminating loops. For instance, instead of looping through each element in an array to perform a calculation, you can perform the operation on the entire array in one go.

```
arr = np.array([1, 2, 3, 4, 5])
# Instead of looping through elements:
```

```
arr = arr * 2
```

This approach is much faster and more efficient, especially when dealing with large datasets.

Leveraging Built-in Functions

Both Numpy and Pandas come with a wide range of built-in functions optimized for performance. Leveraging these functions rather than writing custom code can make your machine learning projects more efficient. For instance, using pandas built-in functions to filter or aggregate data is faster than writing manual loops or list comprehensions.

```
# Using Pandas built-in function to filter data
filtered_df = df[df['Age'] > 20]
```

Memory Management

Handling large datasets efficiently requires careful memory management. Numpy and Pandas allow you to specify data types for arrays and DataFrames, which can help save memory when dealing with large datasets.

For example, specifying data types in Pandas:

```
df = pd.read_csv('data.csv', dtype={'Age': 'int32', 'Salary': 'float32'})
```

By specifying smaller data types, you can reduce the memory footprint of your DataFrame.

Python's rich ecosystem of libraries—particularly Numpy, Pandas, and Matplotlib—provides the foundation for machine learning development. By mastering these essential concepts, you will be well-equipped to handle the data preprocessing, analysis, and visualization tasks that are crucial to building efficient and effective machine learning models. Whether you're preparing data for training or evaluating the performance of your model, these tools will be invaluable in navigating the machine learning landscape.

Chapter 3

Data Preparation and Feature Engineering

Data preparation is one of the most crucial steps in any machine learning project. A well-prepared dataset not only improves the performance of models but also makes them more generalizable. In this chapter, we will explore the key processes involved in preparing data for machine learning models. This includes handling missing data, scaling features, transforming variables, and optimizing the feature set through feature selection and extraction. Scikit-Learn offers a variety of preprocessing utilities that make these tasks easier and more efficient, allowing you to prepare your datasets effectively.

The Importance of Data Preparation

Data in its raw form is rarely ready for machine learning. It may have missing values, irrelevant information, or features that need scaling and transformation. Without proper data preparation, machine learning models may perform poorly or give misleading results. Poorly scaled features, for instance, can lead to biases in distance-based algorithms, while unhandled missing data can break the training process.

There are three primary steps in data preparation:

- **Cleaning the data**: Handling missing values, duplicates, and errors.
- **Transforming the data**: Scaling, normalizing, or encoding categorical variables.
- **Optimizing the data**: Selecting and engineering features that will help the model learn better.

Handling Missing Data

One of the most common problems in datasets is missing data. Missing values can occur due to various reasons, such as data collection errors or incomplete surveys. It's important to address these issues, as models cannot handle missing data directly.

There are several strategies for dealing with missing values:

- **Remove Missing Values**: In some cases, you can remove rows or columns with missing data. This approach is suitable when the percentage of missing values is low, and removing them won't compromise the integrity of the dataset.
- **Imputation**: A more common approach is to fill in missing values with reasonable estimates, such as the mean, median, or mode for numerical features. For categorical features, you might use the most frequent category or a special label such as "Unknown."

In Scikit-Learn, you can use the SimpleImputer class to handle missing values easily.

```
from sklearn.impute import SimpleImputer
import numpy as np

# Create a SimpleImputer instance
imputer = SimpleImputer(strategy='mean')

# Fit and transform the data
imputed_data = imputer.fit_transform(data)
```

For categorical variables, a strategy like imputing the mode (most frequent value) is often effective:

```
imputer = SimpleImputer(strategy='most_frequent')
imputed_data                                     =
imputer.fit_transform(categorical_data)
```

Advanced Imputation Techniques

For more complex datasets, advanced imputation methods like **K-Nearest Neighbors (KNN) Imputation** or **Multivariate Imputation by Chained Equations (MICE)** can be used. These approaches predict missing values by taking into account the relationships between features, improving the quality of the imputed data.

Scaling Features

Feature scaling is a critical step in data preparation, especially for algorithms that rely on distance calculations, such as K-Nearest Neighbors (KNN), Support Vector Machines (SVMs), or gradient descent-based algorithms like linear regression. If features are on different scales, models may give undue importance to certain features.

There are two common scaling methods:

- **Normalization**: This technique scales the data so that it has a range between 0 and 1.
- **Standardization**: Standardization centers the data by subtracting the mean and scaling by the standard deviation, resulting in a distribution with a mean of 0 and a standard deviation of 1.

In Scikit-Learn, the StandardScaler and MinMaxScaler classes provide easy methods for scaling.

```
from sklearn.preprocessing import StandardScaler, MinMaxScaler

# Standardization
scaler = StandardScaler()
scaled_data = scaler.fit_transform(data)

# Normalization
min_max_scaler = MinMaxScaler()
normalized_data = min_max_scaler.fit_transform(data)
```

Encoding Categorical Variables

Many machine learning algorithms work best with numerical input. However, real-world datasets often contain categorical variables, such as gender, city, or product type. These variables need to be encoded before being fed into machine learning models.

One-Hot Encoding

One of the most common methods for encoding categorical data is **One-Hot Encoding**, which creates a new binary column for each category. For example, if you have a "Country" feature with values "USA," "Canada," and "Mexico," One-Hot Encoding will create three new columns, one for each country.

```
from sklearn.preprocessing import OneHotEncoder

# Create a OneHotEncoder instance
encoder = OneHotEncoder()

# Fit and transform the data
encoded_data                          =
encoder.fit_transform(categorical_data)
```

Label Encoding

For ordinal categorical data (where the categories have an inherent order), **Label Encoding** can be used. This assigns a unique integer to each category based on its rank. For example, "Low," "Medium," and "High" can be assigned values 0, 1, and 2, respectively.

```
from sklearn.preprocessing import LabelEncoder

# Create a LabelEncoder instance
label_encoder = LabelEncoder()

# Fit and transform the data
encoded_labels                              =
label_encoder.fit_transform(categorical_data)
```

Feature Engineering: Transforming Variables

Feature engineering is the process of transforming raw data into features that better represent the underlying patterns to the machine learning model. This can involve creating new features from existing ones, transforming variables into more informative representations, or extracting important features from the raw data.

Log Transformation

Log transformations are often used to make highly skewed data more normal. This is particularly useful for models that assume the data follows a normal distribution, such as linear regression.

For example:

```
import numpy as np

# Apply log transformation
log_transformed = np.log(data + 1)
```

Polynomial Features

For models that require non-linear relationships, you can create polynomial features, which are combinations of the original features raised to different powers. This is especially useful for linear models to capture non-linear patterns.

Scikit-Learn offers the PolynomialFeatures class to automate this process.

```
from sklearn.preprocessing import PolynomialFeatures

# Create polynomial features
poly = PolynomialFeatures(degree=2)
polynomial_data = poly.fit_transform(data)
```

Binning and Discretization

Binning is another technique for transforming continuous data into discrete intervals, which can simplify the model's task or reduce the effect of outliers. Binning can be useful when dealing with features like age or income, where grouping values into ranges makes sense.

In Scikit-Learn, you can use KBinsDiscretizer for this purpose.

```
from sklearn.preprocessing import KBinsDiscretizer

# Create bins
binner = KBinsDiscretizer(n_bins=5, encode='ordinal')
binned_data = binner.fit_transform(data)
```

Feature Selection: Choosing the Right Features

Selecting the right features is critical for building efficient and interpretable machine learning models. Irrelevant or redundant features can lead to overfitting and unnecessarily complex models, while the right set of features can improve model performance and reduce computational cost.

There are several techniques for feature selection:

- **Univariate Feature Selection**: This approach evaluates each feature independently using statistical tests to determine its relevance.
- **Recursive Feature Elimination (RFE)**: RFE recursively removes the least important features, training the model each time until the optimal set of features is reached.
- **L1 Regularization (Lasso)**: L1 regularization adds a penalty for large feature weights, effectively

eliminating irrelevant features by assigning them a weight of zero.

In Scikit-Learn, you can use the SelectKBest class for univariate feature selection.

```
from sklearn.feature_selection import SelectKBest, chi2

# Select the top 10 features based on the chi-squared test
selector = SelectKBest(score_func=chi2, k=10)
selected_features = selector.fit_transform(data, labels)
```

Feature Extraction: Dimensionality Reduction

Feature extraction refers to creating new features from the existing ones, usually through dimensionality reduction. This is often necessary when dealing with high-dimensional datasets, where a large number of features can lead to overfitting and slow model training.

Principal Component Analysis (PCA)

One of the most popular methods for dimensionality reduction is **Principal Component Analysis (PCA)**. PCA reduces the number of features by transforming the data into a set of uncorrelated components that capture the maximum variance.

In Scikit-Learn, PCA can be applied as follows:

```
from sklearn.decomposition import PCA

# Create a PCA instance and reduce the data to 2
components
pca = PCA(n_components=2)
pca_data = pca.fit_transform(data)
```

Linear Discriminant Analysis (LDA)

Another method is **Linear Discriminant Analysis (LDA)**, which aims to maximize the separation between different classes in the data. LDA is particularly useful for classification problems.

```
from      sklearn.discriminant_analysis      import
LinearDiscriminantAnalysis as LDA

# Create an LDA instance and reduce the data
lda = LDA(n_components=1)
lda_data = lda.fit_transform(data, labels)
```

Data preparation and feature engineering are foundational steps in the machine learning pipeline. Properly prepared data ensures that models perform at their best and generalize well to unseen data. Scikit-Learn's robust set of utilities simplifies many aspects of data preparation, from handling missing values to transforming variables and selecting the right features. By mastering these techniques, you will be able to build more accurate and efficient machine learning models

Chapter 4

Understanding Supervised Learning Algorithms

Supervised learning is one of the most fundamental and widely used techniques in machine learning. At its core, it involves training a model using labeled data—data where both the input features and the corresponding target labels are known. The goal is to learn a mapping from inputs to outputs so that the model can predict the labels for new, unseen data. Supervised learning is particularly powerful for tasks such as classification and regression, where the relationship between the input features and the output labels is relatively clear.

This chapter explores the fundamental supervised learning algorithms such as linear regression, decision trees, and nearest neighbors. Each of these algorithms has its strengths, limitations, and specific use cases, and Scikit-Learn provides intuitive interfaces for implementing them in Python.

The Concept of Supervised Learning

Supervised learning is based on the idea of learning from examples. A dataset used in supervised learning consists of input-output pairs where each input (or feature) corresponds to a particular output (or label). The objective of supervised learning is to train a model that can accurately predict the output for new inputs by identifying patterns in the training data.

The two major types of supervised learning tasks are:

- **Classification**: Predicting a discrete label or category (e.g., classifying emails as spam or not spam).
- **Regression**: Predicting a continuous value (e.g., forecasting house prices).

The process generally involves the following steps:

1. **Data Collection**: Gathering the labeled dataset.
2. **Model Selection**: Choosing an appropriate supervised learning algorithm.
3. **Training**: Feeding the training data into the model and allowing it to learn from the data.
4. **Evaluation**: Testing the model's performance on a separate test set to see how well it generalizes to unseen data.

Linear Regression

Linear regression is one of the simplest and most interpretable supervised learning algorithms used for regression tasks. It attempts to model the relationship between one or more input variables (also called predictors or features) and an output variable (or target) by fitting a linear equation to the observed data. In essence, linear regression finds the best-fitting straight line through the data points.

Mathematics Behind Linear Regression

The linear regression model can be expressed as:

y=β0+β1x1+β2x2+⋯+βnxn+εy = \beta_0 + \beta_1 x_1 + \beta_2 x_2 + \dots + \beta_n x_n + \epsilony=β0+β1 x1+β2x2+⋯+βnxn+ε

Here, yyy is the target variable, x1,x2,…,xnx_1, x_2, \dots, x_nx1,x2,…,xn are the features, β0\beta_0β0 is the intercept, and β1,β2,…,βn\beta_1, \beta_2, \dots, \beta_nβ1,β2,…,βn are the coefficients. The term ε\epsilonε represents the residual error (the difference between the actual and predicted values).

The goal of linear regression is to estimate the coefficients β1,β2,…,βn\beta_1, \beta_2, \dots, \beta_nβ1,β2,…,βn that minimize the sum of squared residuals. This is done through a method called **Ordinary Least Squares (OLS)**.

Implementing Linear Regression in Scikit-Learn

Scikit-Learn's LinearRegression class allows for quick and efficient implementation of linear regression.

```
from sklearn.linear_model import LinearRegression

# Define the model
model = LinearRegression()
```

```
# Train the model
model.fit(X_train, y_train)

# Make predictions
predictions = model.predict(X_test)
```

Linear regression works well when there is a linear relationship between the features and the target. However, it may struggle with more complex relationships, where non-linear models may perform better.

Decision Trees

Decision trees are a versatile algorithm used for both classification and regression tasks. A decision tree splits the data into smaller and smaller subsets based on feature values, creating a tree-like structure. The decision-making process is guided by questions about the features, such as "Is feature X greater than value Y?" These questions lead to branches in the tree, ultimately ending in leaf nodes that represent the predicted outcome.

How Decision Trees Work

Decision trees are built by recursively splitting the data into smaller subsets based on the feature that results in the greatest reduction in impurity. For classification tasks, this impurity can be measured using metrics such as **Gini impurity** or **Entropy**, while for regression tasks, the variance within subsets is minimized.

For example, in classification, the decision tree starts at the root node with the entire dataset. It evaluates all possible splits on each feature to determine the one that best separates the data into distinct classes. This process continues until each node contains data points from only one class (pure nodes) or another stopping criterion is met.

Implementing Decision Trees in Scikit-Learn

Scikit-Learn provides the DecisionTreeClassifier and DecisionTreeRegressor classes for implementing decision trees for classification and regression tasks, respectively.

```
from sklearn.tree import DecisionTreeClassifier

# Define the model
clf = DecisionTreeClassifier()

# Train the model
clf.fit(X_train, y_train)

# Make predictions
predictions = clf.predict(X_test)
```

Decision trees are intuitive and easy to interpret. However, they are prone to overfitting, particularly when they grow too deep. Techniques like **pruning** (limiting the depth of the tree) or using ensemble methods like Random Forests (covered in a later chapter) can help mitigate this issue.

K-Nearest Neighbors (KNN)

The K-Nearest Neighbors (KNN) algorithm is a simple yet powerful method for both classification and regression. Unlike many other algorithms, KNN is an **instance-based learning** method, meaning it does not learn an explicit model during training. Instead, it stores the training data and makes predictions based on the proximity of a new instance to its nearest neighbors in the training set.

How KNN Works

To classify a new data point, KNN looks at the K nearest data points in the training set and assigns the class that appears most frequently among those neighbors. For regression tasks, KNN predicts the average value of the K nearest neighbors.

Choosing the right value of K is important. A small K (e.g., K=1) may result in a model that is too sensitive to noise in the data, while a large K may smooth out important distinctions between classes.

Implementing KNN in Scikit-Learn

Scikit-Learn's KNeighborsClassifier and KNeighborsRegressor provide implementations for classification and regression, respectively.

```
from sklearn.neighbors import KNeighborsClassifier

# Define the model
knn = KNeighborsClassifier(n_neighbors=3)

# Train the model
knn.fit(X_train, y_train)

# Make predictions
predictions = knn.predict(X_test)
```

KNN works well with smaller datasets and simple classification tasks but can become computationally expensive as the dataset grows, since it has to compute the distance to every training point for each prediction.

Model Evaluation in Supervised Learning

A critical aspect of supervised learning is evaluating the performance of the trained model. This involves comparing the predicted outputs with the true outputs in a test dataset. Common evaluation metrics include:

- **Accuracy**: The proportion of correct predictions (useful for classification).

- **Mean Squared Error (MSE)**: The average of the squared differences between predicted and true values (useful for regression).
- **Precision and Recall**: Precision measures the proportion of true positives among the predicted positives, while recall measures the proportion of true positives among the actual positives (important for imbalanced classification problems).

In Scikit-Learn, you can easily compute these metrics using built-in functions like accuracy_score or mean_squared_error.

```
from sklearn.metrics import accuracy_score

# Calculate accuracy
accuracy = accuracy_score(y_test, predictions)
```

By understanding and selecting the appropriate supervised learning algorithm, you can solve a wide range of machine learning problems. Each algorithm has its own advantages and limitations, and the choice of algorithm often depends on the nature of the dataset and the specific task at hand.

Supervised learning algorithms form the backbone of machine learning. From simple linear regression to decision trees and K-Nearest Neighbors, these algorithms are versatile and effective for a wide range of applications. With Scikit-Learn, implementing these algorithms becomes a straightforward process, allowing machine learning practitioners to focus on fine-tuning their models and improving performance.

Chapter 5

Building and Evaluating Regression Models

Regression models are essential in predicting continuous values based on input features. Unlike classification models, which predict discrete categories, regression models focus on estimating relationships between variables to predict numerical outcomes. The ability to create accurate and reliable regression models is vital for many fields, including finance, healthcare, and social sciences, where the goal is often to forecast future values or understand the strength of the relationship between variables.

In this chapter, we will delve into building regression models using Scikit-Learn, covering both simple and multiple regression models. We will also explore performance evaluation methods to ensure that the models not only fit the data well but also generalize effectively to unseen data. Evaluation metrics like Mean Squared Error (MSE) and R^2 scores play a critical role in assessing the quality of regression models.

Introduction to Regression Analysis

At its core, regression analysis is about modeling the relationship between a dependent variable (also called the target or response) and one or more independent variables (also known as features or predictors). The goal is to find a function that best explains how the target variable changes as the input features vary. This relationship is typically expressed as:

$$y=f(X)+\epsilon y = f(X) + \text{\epsilon} y=f(X)+\epsilon$$

Where yyy is the dependent variable, XXX represents the input features, $f(X)f(X)f(X)$ is the function representing the relationship between XXX and yyy, and $\epsilon\text{\epsilon}\epsilon$ is the error term or residual, accounting for any unexplained variation in the target variable.

Regression analysis helps to uncover trends, quantify relationships between variables, and make predictions for future data points.

Simple Linear Regression

Simple linear regression is one of the most basic forms of regression analysis. It models the relationship between two variables: one independent variable (feature) and one dependent variable (target). The relationship is modeled as a straight line, which is why it is called linear regression.

The equation for simple linear regression is given by:

$$y=\beta 0+\beta 1 x+\epsilon y = \text{\beta\_0} + \text{\beta\_1} x + \text{\epsilon} y=\beta 0+\beta 1 x+\epsilon$$

Where:

- $y$$y$$y$ is the predicted target value.
- $x$$x$$x$ is the input feature.
- β_0\beta_0β_0 is the intercept (the value of $y$$y$$y$ when $x=0$$x = 0$$x=0$).
- β_1\beta_1β_1 is the slope (the change in $y$$y$$y$ for a unit change in $x$$x$$x$).
- ϵ\epsilon$\epsilon$ is the residual error.

Building Simple Linear Regression Models in Scikit-Learn

Scikit-Learn makes it easy to implement simple linear regression using the LinearRegression class.

```
from sklearn.linear_model import LinearRegression

# Define the model
model = LinearRegression()

# Fit the model to the training data
model.fit(X_train, y_train)

# Make predictions
y_pred = model.predict(X_test)
```

After fitting the model, you can interpret the coefficient β_1\beta_1β_1, which represents the effect of the feature $x$$x$$x$ on the target $y$$y$$y$. For example, in a model predicting house prices, β_1\beta_1β_1 might represent the price increase for each additional square foot of space.

Multiple Linear Regression

Multiple linear regression extends simple linear regression by modeling the relationship between a dependent variable and multiple independent variables. This is more realistic for many real-world scenarios, where the target depends on more than just one feature.

The equation for multiple linear regression is:

$$y = \beta_0 + \beta_1 x_1 + \beta_2 x_2 + \dots + \beta_n x_n + \epsilon$$

Where $x_1, x_2, \dots, x_n$ are the input features, and $\beta_1, \beta_2, \dots, \beta_n$ are the corresponding coefficients. Each coefficient represents the contribution of its respective feature to the predicted value.

Building Multiple Linear Regression Models in Scikit-Learn

The process of building a multiple regression model in Scikit-Learn is similar to that of simple linear regression. The difference lies in the number of input features.

```
from sklearn.linear_model import LinearRegression

# Define the model
```

```
model = LinearRegression()

# Fit the model to the training data with multiple
features
model.fit(X_train, y_train)

# Make predictions
y_pred = model.predict(X_test)
```

In multiple regression, the coefficients $\beta_1, \beta_2, \dots, \beta_n$\beta_1, \beta_2, \dots, \beta_n$\beta_1, \beta_2, \dots, \beta_n$ provide insights into the importance of each feature. However, the interpretation can become more complex, especially when the features are correlated.

Evaluating Regression Models

Building a regression model is only the first step. To determine if a model performs well, you must evaluate its performance. This involves comparing the predicted values y_{pred}y_{\text{pred}}y_{pred} against the actual values y_{true}y_{\text{true}}y_{true} from a test set. Several metrics are commonly used to assess the quality of a regression model.

Mean Squared Error (MSE)

One of the most widely used metrics for regression problems is the **Mean Squared Error (MSE)**. MSE measures the average squared difference between the predicted values and the actual values:

$$MSE = \frac{1}{n} \sum_{i=1}^{n} (y_i - \hat{y}_i)^2$$

Where n is the number of data points, y_i is the actual value, and $\hat{y}_i$ is the predicted value. The MSE penalizes larger errors more than smaller ones, making it a good measure of overall model performance. A lower MSE indicates a better model.

You can calculate MSE in Scikit-Learn using the mean_squared_error function.

```
from sklearn.metrics import mean_squared_error

# Calculate MSE
mse = mean_squared_error(y_test, y_pred)
```

Root Mean Squared Error (RMSE)

The **Root Mean Squared Error (RMSE)** is the square root of the MSE. Since MSE is measured in squared units of the target variable, RMSE transforms it back into the original units, making it easier to interpret:

$$RMSE = \sqrt{MSE}$$

59

A lower RMSE value signifies a model that better fits the data. It is often used alongside MSE for regression model evaluation.

```
import numpy as np

# Calculate RMSE
rmse = np.sqrt(mse)
```

R² Score (Coefficient of Determination)

The **R² score**, or **coefficient of determination**, is a measure of how well the independent variables explain the variability in the dependent variable. It ranges from 0 to 1, where a value of 1 indicates that the model perfectly predicts the target values, while a value of 0 means the model performs no better than a simple mean of the target values.

The formula for R² is:

$$R2=1-SSresSStotR^2 \qquad = \qquad 1 \qquad - \text{\textbackslash frac}\{SS\_\{res\}\}\{SS\_\{tot\}\}R2=1-SStotSSres$$

Where:

- SSresSS_{res}SSres is the sum of squares of residuals (i.e., the difference between actual and predicted values).

- $SStot$ SS_{tot}SStot is the total sum of squares (i.e., the difference between actual values and their mean).

A higher R^2 score indicates that the model explains more of the variance in the target variable.

You can calculate the R^2 score using Scikit-Learn's r2_score function.

from sklearn.metrics import r2_score

# Calculate R² score
r2 = r2_score(y_test, y_pred)

Regularization in Regression

One of the challenges of building regression models, especially with multiple features, is overfitting. Overfitting occurs when a model fits the training data too well, capturing noise and outliers, which negatively impacts its performance on unseen data.

Regularization techniques add a penalty to the model's complexity, discouraging it from fitting the training data too closely. Two common types of regularization for linear regression models are:

- **Lasso Regression**: Adds a penalty equal to the absolute value of the coefficients.

- **Ridge Regression**: Adds a penalty equal to the square of the coefficients.

Scikit-Learn provides built-in support for regularization through the Lasso and Ridge classes, allowing you to prevent overfitting and improve model generalization.

Using Cross-Validation for Model Evaluation

Another effective method for evaluating regression models is **cross-validation**. Instead of relying on a single training and test set, cross-validation splits the data into multiple folds. The model is trained on several folds and tested on the remaining fold, rotating through all the data. This provides a more robust estimate of model performance.

Scikit-Learn makes cross-validation easy with the cross_val_score function.

```
from sklearn.model_selection import cross_val_score

# Perform cross-validation
scores = cross_val_score(model, X, y, cv=5)
```

Cross-validation helps ensure that the model is not overfitting or underfitting and gives a more realistic estimate of its performance.

Building and evaluating regression models is a crucial step in developing predictive models that deliver reliable results. Whether using simple or multiple linear regression, understanding how to evaluate your models using metrics like MSE and R^2 scores helps ensure that they generalize well to new data. By incorporating regularization techniques and cross-validation, you can further improve the performance and robustness of your models. Scikit-Learn provides all the tools necessary to implement these concepts, allowing you to focus on refining your models and improving their predictions.

Chapter 6

Classification Algorithms: Logistic Regression, KNN, and Naive Bayes

Classification algorithms are fundamental to machine learning, particularly when dealing with problems that require categorizing data into discrete labels or groups. Unlike regression, which predicts continuous values, classification focuses on predicting categorical outcomes, often in binary (two classes) or multiclass (more than two classes) scenarios. In this chapter, we will explore three widely used classification algorithms: logistic regression, K-nearest neighbors (KNN), and Naive Bayes. These algorithms offer distinct advantages for various types of data, and their implementation is made accessible through Scikit-Learn.

Introduction to Classification in Machine Learning

Classification tasks aim to predict which category or class a new data point belongs to based on the features provided. These types of tasks are common across a wide range of industries and use cases, including spam detection, medical diagnosis, customer segmentation, and sentiment analysis. Each classification algorithm operates differently but shares the same goal of minimizing classification errors and maximizing accuracy.

A classification algorithm learns from labeled data, where the input features and the corresponding labels (categories) are provided. The algorithm builds a model to predict labels for new, unseen data points.

Logistic Regression: Binary and Multiclass Classification

Logistic regression is a popular algorithm for classification problems, especially in binary classification, where the outcome is one of two possible categories. Despite its name, logistic regression is a classification algorithm, not a regression technique. It models the probability of a data point belonging to a particular class using a logistic function (also known as the sigmoid function).

The sigmoid function maps any real-valued number into a value between 0 and 1, representing the probability that a particular data point belongs to class 1. The decision boundary for classification is often set at 0.5, meaning if the probability is greater than 0.5, the model predicts class 1; otherwise, it predicts class 0.

The logistic function is defined as:

$$P(y=1|x) = \frac{1}{1 + e^{-z}}$$

Where $z = \beta_0 + \beta_1 x_1 + \beta_2 x_2 + \dots + \beta_n x_n$

$+\beta 1x1+\beta 2x2+\cdots+\beta nxn$ is the linear combination of the input features and their corresponding coefficients.

Implementing Logistic Regression in Scikit-Learn

Logistic regression in Scikit-Learn is implemented using the LogisticRegression class. It can handle both binary and multiclass classification problems, making it versatile for a wide range of tasks.

```
from sklearn.linear_model import LogisticRegression

# Define the model
model = LogisticRegression()

# Train the model
model.fit(X_train, y_train)

# Make predictions
y_pred = model.predict(X_test)
```

Logistic regression is particularly effective when the classes are linearly separable. It provides probabilistic interpretations and is easy to implement, but it may struggle with more complex, non-linear relationships between the features and the target.

Multiclass Logistic Regression

For multiclass classification problems, Scikit-Learn automatically handles this using a "one-vs-rest" (OvR) strategy by default. OvR trains multiple binary classifiers, one for each class, and then selects the class with the highest probability for each data point. Alternatively, the "multinomial" strategy can be used, which handles multiple classes directly.

To implement multiclass logistic regression, you only need to specify the multi_class parameter in the LogisticRegression class:

model = LogisticRegression(multi_class='multinomial', solver='lbfgs')

This allows logistic regression to handle problems with more than two classes effectively.

K-Nearest Neighbors (KNN): Instance-Based Learning

K-nearest neighbors (KNN) is a simple yet powerful classification algorithm that relies on the proximity of data points in the feature space. KNN is an instance-based learning algorithm, meaning that it does not explicitly build a model but instead classifies new data points based on their similarity to the training data.

In KNN, a data point is classified by considering the classes of its kkk nearest neighbors. The majority class among these neighbors is assigned to the new data point. The value of kkk (the number of neighbors) is a hyperparameter that can be tuned to optimize the model's performance.

KNN works particularly well in low-dimensional data spaces but can become computationally expensive with high-dimensional data or large datasets, as it needs to calculate the distance between the test point and every point in the training set.

Implementing KNN in Scikit-Learn

Scikit-Learn provides an easy way to implement KNN using the KNeighborsClassifier class. The following code demonstrates how to train and evaluate a KNN model:

```
from sklearn.neighbors import KNeighborsClassifier

# Define the model with k=5
model = KNeighborsClassifier(n_neighbors=5)

# Train the model
model.fit(X_train, y_train)

# Make predictions
y_pred = model.predict(X_test)
```

In KNN, the choice of the distance metric (e.g., Euclidean distance, Manhattan distance) is crucial for performance. The default metric is Euclidean distance, but Scikit-Learn allows you to specify different metrics depending on your problem.

Choosing the Right Value for kkk

One of the key decisions in KNN is selecting the appropriate value for kkk, which determines how many neighbors to consider. A small kkk (e.g., k=1k = 1k=1) may lead to a highly sensitive model prone to overfitting, while a larger kkk may smooth out noise in the data but lead to underfitting.

A common approach to selecting the optimal kkk is to use cross-validation and test different values of kkk, evaluating the model's performance on a validation set.

```
from sklearn.model_selection import GridSearchCV

# Set up a parameter grid for k
param_grid = {'n_neighbors': [3, 5, 7, 9]}

# Use GridSearchCV to find the optimal k
grid_search = GridSearchCV(KNeighborsClassifier(),
param_grid, cv=5)
grid_search.fit(X_train, y_train)

# Optimal value for k
print(grid_search.best_params_)
```

Naive Bayes: Probabilistic Classification

Naive Bayes is a family of classification algorithms based on Bayes' Theorem. The "naive" part of Naive Bayes refers to the assumption that the features are independent of each other given the class label. While this assumption is often unrealistic, Naive Bayes can still perform surprisingly well, especially with text data and high-dimensional datasets.

Bayes' Theorem is expressed as:

$P(y|X)=P(X|y) \cdot P(y)P(X)P(y|X) = \frac{P(X|y) \cdot P(y)}{P(X)}P(y|X)=P(X)P(X|y) \cdot P(y)$

Where:

- $P(y|X)P(y|X)P(y|X)$ is the posterior probability of the class yyy given the feature vector XXX.
- $P(X|y)P(X|y)P(X|y)$ is the likelihood of the feature vector given the class.
- $P(y)P(y)P(y)$ is the prior probability of the class.
- $P(X)P(X)P(X)$ is the probability of the feature vector.

Naive Bayes classifiers are probabilistic, meaning they output probabilities for each class, which allows for a clear understanding of the model's confidence in its predictions.

There are different variants of the Naive Bayes algorithm, including:

- **Gaussian Naive Bayes**: For continuous features assuming a normal distribution.
- **Multinomial Naive Bayes**: Typically used for discrete features, such as word counts in text data.
- **Bernoulli Naive Bayes**: For binary or boolean features.

Implementing Naive Bayes in Scikit-Learn

Scikit-Learn offers several Naive Bayes implementations, including GaussianNB, MultinomialNB, and BernoulliNB. Here is an example of using Gaussian Naive Bayes:

```
from sklearn.naive_bayes import GaussianNB

# Define the model
model = GaussianNB()

# Train the model
model.fit(X_train, y_train)

# Make predictions
y_pred = model.predict(X_test)
```

Naive Bayes is particularly efficient for large datasets and is commonly used for text classification tasks, including spam filtering and sentiment analysis.

Evaluating Classification Models

For classification problems, the performance of a model can be evaluated using several metrics. These metrics help to understand how well the model is predicting the correct class labels and whether it is generalizing well to new data.

Accuracy

Accuracy is the simplest evaluation metric and is defined as the ratio of correctly predicted instances to the total number of instances.

$$\text{Accuracy} = \frac{\text{Correct Predictions}}{\text{Total Predictions}}$$

However, accuracy can be misleading, especially in cases where the data is imbalanced (i.e., one class significantly outnumbers the other). In such cases, other metrics like precision, recall, and F1-score are more informative.

Precision, Recall, and F1-Score

Precision measures the proportion of correctly predicted positive instances out of all instances predicted as positive, while recall measures the proportion of correctly predicted positive instances out of all actual positive instances.

$$\text{Precision} = \frac{\text{True Positives}}{\text{True Positives} + \text{False Positives}}$$

$$\text{Recall} = \frac{\text{True Positives}}{\text{True Positives} + \text{False Negatives}}$$

The F1-score is the harmonic mean of precision and recall and is useful for imbalanced datasets.

$$F1 = 2 \cdot \frac{\text{Precision} \cdot \text{Recall}}{\text{Precision} + \text{Recall}}$$

These metrics can be calculated using Scikit-Learn's classification_report function.

```
from sklearn.metrics import classification_report

print(classification_report(y_test, y_pred))
```

Logistic regression, K-nearest neighbors, and Naive Bayes are foundational classification algorithms that cover a wide range of use cases. Whether working with linear relationships, instance-based learning, or probabilistic modeling, each algorithm offers unique strengths. By understanding their inner workings and implementation, machine learning practitioners can effectively apply these models to binary and multiclass classification tasks with confidence.

Chapter 7

Support Vector Machines: Mastering Linear and Nonlinear Classification

Support Vector Machines (SVMs) are a powerful set of supervised learning algorithms commonly used for both classification and regression tasks. Their ability to handle both linear and nonlinear data, along with their effectiveness in high-dimensional spaces, has made them a popular choice for machine learning practitioners. This chapter will delve into the theory behind SVMs, their mathematical foundations, and their practical implementation for classification tasks using Scikit-Learn. We will also explore how to optimize the performance of SVMs by tuning critical parameters such as kernels, regularization, and margin.

Understanding the Basics of Support Vector Machines

At its core, a Support Vector Machine aims to find the best decision boundary (hyperplane) that separates data points into different classes. For a binary classification problem, the SVM algorithm seeks to draw a line or hyperplane that maximizes the margin between the classes. The margin is the distance between the hyperplane and the closest data points from each class, which are known as support vectors.

A key goal of SVMs is to not only separate the classes but to do so with the largest possible margin, thereby making the classifier more robust to new, unseen data. If the classes are not perfectly separable, SVMs can introduce a "soft margin" to allow for some misclassification, balancing the trade-off between maximizing the margin and minimizing classification errors.

The SVM Optimization Problem

The optimization process for an SVM involves solving for the hyperplane that maximizes the margin between the classes. For a binary classification problem with labeled data $(x_i, y_i)(x\_i, \quad y\_i)(x_i, y_i)$, where $y_i \in \{+1, -1\} y\_i \in \{+1, -1\} y_i \in \{+1, -1\}$, the goal is to find a hyperplane that separates the positive and negative classes. The equation of a hyperplane in an SVM is:

$$wTx + b = 0 w^T x + b = 0 wTx + b = 0$$

Where:

- www is the weight vector perpendicular to the hyperplane.
- bbb is the bias or offset from the origin.
- xxx is the feature vector.

The optimization problem is to maximize the margin, subject to constraints that ensure data points are classified correctly:

$y_i(w^T x_i + b) \geq 1$ for all $y_i(w^T x_i + b) \geq 1 \quad \text{for all} \quad i$ $y_i(w^T x_i + b) \geq 1$ for all i

The margin is $\frac{2}{\|w\|}$ $\|w\|2$, so the objective is to minimize $\|w\|2\|w\|^2\|w\|2$, while ensuring that the data points are classified correctly. In the case of nonlinear separability, SVM introduces a "soft margin" controlled by a regularization parameter CCC.

Linear SVM: Separating Linearly Separable Data

In cases where the data is linearly separable, a linear SVM can be used to find the optimal hyperplane that separates the classes with the maximum margin. Linear SVMs work best when the data can be divided by a straight line (in 2D) or a hyperplane (in higher dimensions). The decision boundary found by the SVM ensures that the support vectors are positioned as far away as possible from the hyperplane, leading to a more generalizable model.

Implementing Linear SVM in Scikit-Learn

Scikit-Learn provides a simple interface for implementing linear SVMs through the SVC class, where the kernel is set to 'linear'. Here's an example of how to use a linear SVM for classification:

```
from sklearn.svm import SVC

# Define the model with a linear kernel
model = SVC(kernel='linear')

# Train the model
model.fit(X_train, y_train)

# Make predictions
y_pred = model.predict(X_test)
```

Linear SVMs are effective for problems where the classes are well-separated by a straight line or plane. However, in real-world applications, the data is often not linearly separable. This is where nonlinear SVMs and the concept of kernels come into play.

Nonlinear SVM: Using Kernels for Complex Decision Boundaries

When the data is not linearly separable, SVMs can still perform well by using a technique called the "kernel trick." Kernels allow SVMs to operate in a higher-dimensional space without explicitly computing the coordinates in that space, making it computationally efficient. The idea is to map the original feature space into a higher-dimensional space where the data can be linearly separated.

Popular kernel functions include:

- **Linear kernel**: For linearly separable data.
- **Polynomial kernel**: Captures polynomial relationships between features.
- **Radial Basis Function (RBF) kernel**: Popular for capturing non-linear relationships.
- **Sigmoid kernel**: Similar to neural networks, often less effective than RBF.

The kernel function determines the shape of the decision boundary. For example, the RBF kernel can create complex, curved decision boundaries, making it particularly useful for data that exhibits nonlinear relationships.

Implementing Nonlinear SVM in Scikit-Learn

In Scikit-Learn, you can implement nonlinear SVMs by specifying the desired kernel function in the SVC class. Here's how to use the RBF kernel for a nonlinear classification problem:

```
from sklearn.svm import SVC

# Define the model with an RBF kernel
model = SVC(kernel='rbf')
```

```
# Train the model
model.fit(X_train, y_train)

# Make predictions
y_pred = model.predict(X_test)
```

The choice of kernel function can significantly impact the performance of the SVM model. The RBF kernel is a popular default choice because it works well in many situations, but it's important to experiment with different kernels based on the specific nature of your data.

Tuning Parameters for Optimal SVM Performance

SVMs have several important parameters that can be tuned to improve performance, especially when dealing with complex datasets. The most critical parameters include:

- **C (Regularization Parameter)**: Controls the trade-off between maximizing the margin and allowing for classification errors. A smaller CCC value creates a wider margin but allows more misclassifications, while a larger CCC value creates a narrower margin with fewer misclassifications.
- **Kernel**: Determines the decision boundary. The choice of kernel should match the underlying structure of the data (linear, polynomial, RBF, etc.).

- **Gamma**: Controls the influence of individual data points in the RBF kernel. A small gamma value means that distant points have more influence, while a larger gamma value focuses on closer points.

Tuning SVM Hyperparameters with GridSearchCV

To find the optimal values for the CCC, gamma, and kernel parameters, we can use Scikit-Learn's GridSearchCV, which automates the process of trying different parameter combinations and finding the best-performing model.

```python
from sklearn.model_selection import GridSearchCV
from sklearn.svm import SVC

# Define the parameter grid
param_grid = {
    'C': [0.1, 1, 10, 100],
    'gamma': [1, 0.1, 0.01, 0.001],
    'kernel': ['rbf', 'linear']
}

# Perform grid search
grid = GridSearchCV(SVC(), param_grid, refit=True, verbose=3)
grid.fit(X_train, y_train)

# Best parameters
print(grid.best_params_)
```

```
# Make predictions with the best model
y_pred = grid.predict(X_test)
```

Using GridSearchCV ensures that the model is fine-tuned to your dataset, potentially improving classification accuracy and model robustness.

Support Vectors: Understanding Their Role

In an SVM, not all data points are equally important. Only the data points that lie closest to the decision boundary (the support vectors) influence the position of the hyperplane. These support vectors are the critical elements that define the margin and ultimately determine the classification.

One of the strengths of SVMs is that the decision boundary is defined by only a small subset of the training data, making the algorithm computationally efficient in many scenarios. The support vectors have a significant impact on the final model, and removing them could change the decision boundary entirely.

Visualizing Support Vectors

Scikit-Learn allows you to extract the support vectors from an SVM model, which can then be visualized to understand which data points are most influential in determining the decision boundary.

```
# Extract support vectors
support_vectors = model.support_vectors_

# Plotting support vectors
import matplotlib.pyplot as plt

plt.scatter(X_train[:, 0], X_train[:, 1], c=y_train)
plt.scatter(support_vectors[:, 0], support_vectors[:, 1],
s=100, facecolors='none', edgecolors='r')
plt.show()
```

Advantages and Limitations of SVMs

Advantages:

1. **Effective in High-Dimensional Spaces**: SVMs perform well when the number of features is greater than the number of samples.
2. **Memory Efficiency**: SVMs only use a subset of training data (the support vectors) to create the decision boundary.
3. **Versatile**: SVMs can be used for both linear and nonlinear classification problems using different kernel functions.

Limitations:

1. **Sensitive to Parameter Tuning**: The performance of SVMs depends heavily on the choice of parameters like CCC and gamma. Incorrect tuning can lead to suboptimal performance.

2. **Computationally Expensive**: For large datasets, especially with nonlinear kernels, SVMs can become computationally intensive.
3. **Difficulty with Noisy Data**: SVMs can struggle with noisy data, as outliers can affect the placement of the decision boundary.

Support Vector Machines provide a robust and flexible approach to both linear and nonlinear classification tasks. By understanding the mathematical foundations of SVMs, mastering the implementation of linear and nonlinear models, and learning how to tune critical parameters like CCC, gamma, and the kernel, machine learning practitioners can leverage SVMs to achieve high-performance models for a wide range of applications.

Chapter 8

Decision Trees and Random Forests for Classification and Regression

Decision trees and random forests are two of the most versatile and powerful algorithms in machine learning. Decision trees provide an intuitive model structure by splitting data based on features, while random forests enhance decision trees' performance through ensemble methods. In this chapter, we will delve into the core concepts of decision tree algorithms, understand their strengths and weaknesses, and explore how random forests can be used to improve model accuracy and robustness. By the end of this chapter, you will be able to implement both algorithms for classification and regression tasks using Scikit-Learn.

Understanding Decision Trees

A decision tree is a flowchart-like structure where each internal node represents a decision based on a feature, each branch represents an outcome of the decision, and each leaf node represents a class label (in classification) or a value (in regression). Decision trees are one of the simplest yet highly interpretable machine learning algorithms. They work by recursively splitting the data into subsets based on the most important features, thereby creating a tree structure.

The splits are made to maximize information gain, meaning that the algorithm chooses the feature and threshold that best separates the data into classes or values. Decision trees are highly effective for both classification and regression tasks because of their ability to handle both categorical and numerical data.

How Decision Trees Work

The basic process of building a decision tree involves:

1. **Selecting the Best Feature**: At each node, the algorithm selects the feature that provides the best split. This selection is based on criteria such as **Gini impurity** or **information gain** (based on entropy) for classification, and **variance reduction** for regression.
2. **Splitting the Data**: The selected feature is used to split the data into two or more subsets.
3. **Recursion**: The process is repeated recursively for each subset, with the algorithm selecting the best feature for the new subset at each step.
4. **Stopping Criterion**: The recursion stops when a stopping criterion is met, such as reaching a maximum depth or when further splits do not significantly improve the model.

Gini Impurity and Information Gain

In classification tasks, decision trees use two main criteria to measure the quality of splits:

- **Gini Impurity**: Measures how often a randomly chosen element from the set would be incorrectly classified if it was randomly labeled according to the distribution of labels in the subset.

Gini=1−∑(pi)2Gini = 1 - \sum (p_i)^2Gini=1−∑(pi)2

Where pip_ipi is the proportion of samples belonging to class iii.

- **Information Gain**: Measures the reduction in entropy after a dataset is split on a feature. The goal is to minimize the entropy in the resulting subsets.

Information Gain=Entropy (parent)−∑(size of childsize of parent)×Entropy (child)\text{Information Gain} = \text{Entropy (parent)} - \sum \left(\frac{\text{size of child}}{\text{size of parent}}\right) \times \text{Entropy (child)}Information Gain=Entropy (parent)−∑(size of parentsize of child)×Entropy (child)

Implementing Decision Trees in Scikit-Learn

Scikit-Learn provides a simple way to implement decision trees using the DecisionTreeClassifier and DecisionTreeRegressor classes. Here's how to implement a decision tree for classification:

```
from sklearn.tree import DecisionTreeClassifier

# Initialize the classifier
```

```
clf = DecisionTreeClassifier()

# Train the model
clf.fit(X_train, y_train)

# Make predictions
y_pred = clf.predict(X_test)
```

For regression, the process is almost identical but uses DecisionTreeRegressor:

```
from sklearn.tree import DecisionTreeRegressor

# Initialize the regressor
reg = DecisionTreeRegressor()

# Train the model
reg.fit(X_train, y_train)

# Make predictions
y_pred = reg.predict(X_test)
```

Strengths and Weaknesses of Decision Trees

Strengths

- **Easy to Interpret**: Decision trees are intuitive and easy to visualize, making them useful for explaining model predictions to non-technical stakeholders.

- **Handles Non-linear Data**: Decision trees can model complex, non-linear relationships between features and labels.
- **No Need for Feature Scaling**: Unlike algorithms such as logistic regression or SVM, decision trees do not require feature scaling.

Weaknesses

- **Prone to Overfitting**: Decision trees can easily overfit the training data, especially when allowed to grow too deep. This can lead to poor generalization on unseen data.
- **Sensitive to Small Changes in Data**: Small changes in the training data can lead to a completely different tree, making them less stable compared to other algorithms.
- **Not the Most Accurate**: While decision trees provide an interpretable model, they are often not the most accurate, particularly in comparison to more complex models like random forests or gradient boosting.

Random Forests: An Ensemble of Decision Trees

Random forests are a powerful extension of decision trees that address many of the weaknesses of individual trees. A random forest is an ensemble learning method that builds multiple decision trees and merges their outputs to produce a more accurate and stable prediction. The key idea behind random forests is that by averaging multiple decision trees, the model reduces variance and improves generalization, thereby mitigating the risk of overfitting.

How Random Forests Work

1. **Bootstrap Aggregating (Bagging)**: The random forest algorithm creates multiple decision trees by bootstrapping, meaning it generates different training datasets by sampling from the original dataset with replacement. This helps to create diverse trees that make different splits based on different subsets of the data.
2. **Random Feature Selection**: At each split in a decision tree, the random forest algorithm selects a random subset of features to consider for splitting the data. This introduces even more variability among the trees, ensuring that the ensemble is not dominated by any particular feature.
3. **Majority Voting for Classification**: Once all the trees have made their predictions, the random forest combines their outputs. For classification tasks, it uses majority voting, where the class that gets the most votes from individual trees becomes the final prediction.
4. **Averaging for Regression**: For regression tasks, the random forest takes the average of the predictions from all the trees to get the final output.

Implementing Random Forests in Scikit-Learn

Like decision trees, random forests can be easily implemented in Scikit-Learn using the RandomForestClassifier for classification and RandomForestRegressor for regression. Here's an example of how to implement a random forest for classification:

```
from sklearn.ensemble import RandomForestClassifier

# Initialize the classifier
clf = RandomForestClassifier(n_estimators=100)

# Train the model
clf.fit(X_train, y_train)

# Make predictions
y_pred = clf.predict(X_test)
```

For regression, you can use RandomForestRegressor:

```
from sklearn.ensemble import RandomForestRegressor

# Initialize the regressor
reg = RandomForestRegressor(n_estimators=100)

# Train the model
reg.fit(X_train, y_train)

# Make predictions
```

```
y_pred = reg.predict(X_test)
```

Tuning Random Forest Hyperparameters

Random forests have several hyperparameters that can be tuned to improve performance:

- **n_estimators**: The number of trees in the forest. More trees generally lead to better performance but increase computational cost.
- **max_depth**: The maximum depth of the trees. Limiting depth can prevent overfitting.
- **min_samples_split**: The minimum number of samples required to split an internal node.
- **min_samples_leaf**: The minimum number of samples required to be at a leaf node.
- **max_features**: The number of features to consider when looking for the best split. By default, this is the square root of the total number of features for classification.

Tuning with GridSearchCV

Scikit-Learn's GridSearchCV can be used to automatically search for the best combination of hyperparameters:

```
from sklearn.model_selection import GridSearchCV
from sklearn.ensemble import RandomForestClassifier
```

```
# Define parameter grid
param_grid = {
    'n_estimators': [100, 200, 300],
    'max_depth': [10, 20, 30],
    'min_samples_split': [2, 5, 10],
    'min_samples_leaf': [1, 2, 4]
}

# Initialize grid search
grid_search                            =
GridSearchCV(RandomForestClassifier(), param_grid,
cv=5)

# Fit model
grid_search.fit(X_train, y_train)

# Best parameters
print(grid_search.best_params_)
```

Advantages and Limitations of Random Forests

Advantages:

1. **Improved Accuracy**: Random forests reduce variance and improve model accuracy compared to individual decision trees.
2. **Resistant to Overfitting**: By averaging the predictions of multiple trees, random forests are less prone to overfitting.

3. **Handles Large Datasets**: Random forests can efficiently handle large datasets with a high number of features.

Limitations:

1. **Interpretability**: While individual decision trees are easy to interpret, random forests, being an ensemble method, lose this interpretability.
2. **Computational Cost**: Training a large number of trees can be computationally expensive and time-consuming.

Decision trees and random forests provide an excellent balance between simplicity and performance in machine learning. Decision trees offer an interpretable and flexible model for both classification and regression, while random forests take this further by reducing variance and improving generalization through ensemble learning. Understanding how to implement and tune these algorithms using Scikit-Learn gives you a powerful toolkit for building robust machine learning models.

Chapter 9

Ensemble Learning: Bagging, Boosting, and Stacking

Ensemble learning techniques are crucial for enhancing the performance and robustness of machine learning models. By combining multiple weak models into a single strong learner, ensemble methods can improve accuracy, reduce overfitting, and create more reliable predictions. In this chapter, we will explore three primary ensemble learning techniques: Bagging, Boosting, and Stacking. We will discuss the principles behind each method, their advantages and limitations, and how to implement them using Scikit-Learn.

Bagging: Bootstrap Aggregating

Bagging, or Bootstrap Aggregating, is an ensemble method that aims to reduce the variance of a machine learning model. The central idea behind bagging is to train multiple instances of the same model on different subsets of the training data and then combine their predictions.

How Bagging Works

1. **Data Sampling**: Multiple bootstrap samples (random subsets with replacement) are created from the original dataset. Each sample is used to train a separate model.

2. **Model Training**: Each model is trained independently on its corresponding bootstrap sample.
3. **Aggregation**: The predictions from all models are combined. For classification tasks, this is typically done through majority voting, while for regression tasks, the average of predictions is used.

Benefits of Bagging

- **Reduction in Variance**: Bagging helps in reducing the variance of the model by averaging out the noise and errors of individual models.
- **Improved Stability**: By training multiple models on different subsets of data, bagging makes the overall model more stable and less sensitive to fluctuations in the training data.
- **Versatility**: Bagging can be applied to various machine learning algorithms, including decision trees, which are commonly used in conjunction with this technique.

Implementing Bagging with Scikit-Learn

Scikit-Learn provides the BaggingClassifier and BaggingRegressor classes to implement bagging. Here's an example of using bagging with a decision tree classifier:

```
from sklearn.ensemble import BaggingClassifier
from sklearn.tree import DecisionTreeClassifier
```

```
# Initialize the base model
base_model = DecisionTreeClassifier()

# Initialize the Bagging Classifier
bagging_model    =    BaggingClassifier(base_model,
n_estimators=50)

# Train the model
bagging_model.fit(X_train, y_train)

# Make predictions
y_pred = bagging_model.predict(X_test)
```

Boosting: Enhancing Model Performance

Boosting is an ensemble method that focuses on converting weak learners into strong learners by sequentially training models, where each new model corrects the errors made by the previous ones. Boosting methods typically emphasize improving model performance by adjusting weights based on previous predictions.

How Boosting Works

1. **Initial Model**: A base model is trained on the original data.
2. **Error Calculation**: The errors or residuals from the initial model are calculated.

3. **Model Training**: A new model is trained on the data with adjusted weights that emphasize the errors made by the previous model.
4. **Iteration**: The process is repeated iteratively, with each new model correcting the mistakes of the previous models.
5. **Aggregation**: The final prediction is made by combining the predictions of all models, often through weighted voting for classification or averaging for regression.

Popular Boosting Algorithms

- **AdaBoost (Adaptive Boosting)**: AdaBoost adjusts the weights of incorrectly classified instances to focus more on challenging cases. Each subsequent model is trained with a higher emphasis on these misclassified examples.
- **Gradient Boosting**: Gradient Boosting builds models sequentially, where each new model tries to minimize the residual errors of the combined ensemble of previous models. It uses gradient descent to optimize the model parameters.

Implementing Boosting with Scikit-Learn

Here's how to implement AdaBoost and Gradient Boosting using Scikit-Learn:

AdaBoost Example:

```python
from sklearn.ensemble import AdaBoostClassifier
from sklearn.tree import DecisionTreeClassifier

# Initialize the base model
base_model = DecisionTreeClassifier(max_depth=1)

# Initialize the AdaBoost Classifier
adaboost_model = AdaBoostClassifier(base_model,
n_estimators=50)

# Train the model
adaboost_model.fit(X_train, y_train)

# Make predictions
y_pred = adaboost_model.predict(X_test)
```

Gradient Boosting Example:

```python
from sklearn.ensemble import
GradientBoostingClassifier

# Initialize the Gradient Boosting Classifier
gb_model =
GradientBoostingClassifier(n_estimators=100,
learning_rate=0.1)

# Train the model
gb_model.fit(X_train, y_train)
```

```
# Make predictions
y_pred = gb_model.predict(X_test)
```

Stacking: Combining Multiple Models

Stacking, or Stacked Generalization, is an ensemble technique that combines multiple models to create a stronger predictive model. Unlike bagging and boosting, which typically use the same type of base model, stacking allows for a diverse set of models to be combined.

How Stacking Works

1. **Base Models**: Multiple base models (which can be different types of models) are trained on the training dataset.
2. **Meta-Model**: A meta-model, or a second-level model, is trained on the outputs of the base models. This meta-model learns how to best combine the predictions from the base models.
3. **Prediction Combination**: For making predictions, the base models generate predictions, which are then used as input features for the meta-model to produce the final prediction.

Implementing Stacking with Scikit-Learn

Scikit-Learn provides the StackingClassifier and StackingRegressor classes to implement stacking.

Here's an example of using stacking with different types of base models:

```python
from sklearn.ensemble import StackingClassifier
from sklearn.linear_model import LogisticRegression
from sklearn.tree import DecisionTreeClassifier
from sklearn.svm import SVC

# Initialize the base models
base_models = [
    ('dt', DecisionTreeClassifier()),
    ('svm', SVC(probability=True))
]

# Initialize the meta-model
meta_model = LogisticRegression()

# Initialize the Stacking Classifier
stacking_model = StackingClassifier(estimators=base_models, final_estimator=meta_model)

# Train the model
stacking_model.fit(X_train, y_train)

# Make predictions
y_pred = stacking_model.predict(X_test)
```

Advantages and Limitations of Ensemble Methods

Advantages:

1. **Improved Accuracy**: Ensemble methods often achieve higher accuracy compared to individual models by leveraging their strengths and mitigating their weaknesses.
2. **Reduction in Overfitting**: Techniques like bagging help to reduce overfitting by combining multiple models.
3. **Versatility**: Ensemble methods can be applied to a wide range of base models and can be adapted to different types of machine learning problems.

Limitations:

1. **Complexity**: Ensemble methods can be complex to implement and tune, especially with large numbers of base models.
2. **Computational Cost**: Training multiple models can be computationally expensive and time-consuming.
3. **Interpretability**: While individual models like decision trees are easy to interpret, ensembles of multiple models can be more challenging to understand.

Ensemble learning techniques such as Bagging, Boosting, and Stacking provide powerful ways to improve machine learning model performance by combining multiple models into a single strong learner. Each technique has its unique advantages and is suited for different types of problems. By understanding and implementing these ensemble methods using Scikit-Learn, you can build more accurate, robust, and reliable machine learning models.

Chapter 10

Unsupervised Learning: Clustering and Dimensionality Reduction

Unsupervised learning is a vital aspect of machine learning that deals with extracting patterns and structures from data without pre-existing labels. This chapter delves into two core unsupervised learning techniques: clustering and dimensionality reduction. We will explore clustering methods such as K-Means, hierarchical clustering, and DBSCAN, as well as dimensionality reduction techniques like Principal Component Analysis (PCA) and t-Distributed Stochastic Neighbor Embedding (t-SNE). Understanding these methods will enable you to uncover hidden patterns and simplify complex datasets.

Clustering: Discovering Natural Groupings

Clustering is a technique used to group similar data points together based on their features. Unlike supervised learning, where the goal is to predict an outcome, clustering aims to identify inherent structures in the data.

K-Means Clustering

K-Means is one of the most widely used clustering algorithms. It partitions data into K distinct clusters, with each cluster represented by its centroid. The algorithm iteratively refines the clusters to minimize the variance within each cluster.

How K-Means Works:

1. **Initialization**: Select K initial centroids randomly from the data points.
2. **Assignment**: Assign each data point to the nearest centroid, forming K clusters.
3. **Update**: Calculate the new centroids by taking the mean of the data points assigned to each cluster.
4. **Repeat**: Repeat the assignment and update steps until the centroids no longer change significantly or a maximum number of iterations is reached.

Advantages:

- **Simplicity**: K-Means is easy to understand and implement.
- **Efficiency**: It is computationally efficient and works well with large datasets.

Limitations:

- **Choosing K**: Determining the optimal number of clusters (K) can be challenging.
- **Assumption of Spherical Clusters**: K-Means assumes clusters are spherical and equally sized, which may not always be true.

Implementing K-Means with Scikit-Learn:

```python
from sklearn.cluster import KMeans

# Initialize K-Means with K clusters
kmeans = KMeans(n_clusters=3)

# Fit the model to the data
kmeans.fit(X)

# Predict the cluster for each data point
clusters = kmeans.predict(X)
```

Hierarchical Clustering

Hierarchical clustering builds a hierarchy of clusters either through a bottom-up approach (agglomerative) or a top-down approach (divisive).

Agglomerative Hierarchical Clustering:

1. **Initialization**: Start with each data point as its own cluster.
2. **Merge**: Iteratively merge the closest clusters until only one cluster remains or a predefined number of clusters is achieved.
3. **Dendrogram**: A dendrogram is used to visualize the hierarchical structure of the clusters.

Advantages:

- **No Need for Predefined K**: The number of clusters does not need to be specified in advance.
- **Hierarchical Structure**: Provides a hierarchy that can be useful for understanding data relationships.

Limitations:

- **Computational Complexity**: Hierarchical clustering can be computationally intensive for large datasets.
- **Sensitivity to Noise**: The algorithm can be sensitive to noise and outliers.

Implementing Hierarchical Clustering with Scikit-Learn:

```
from sklearn.cluster import AgglomerativeClustering

# Initialize Agglomerative Clustering with a specified
number of clusters
agg_clustering                              =
AgglomerativeClustering(n_clusters=3)

# Fit the model to the data
clusters = agg_clustering.fit_predict(X)
```

DBSCAN (Density-Based Spatial Clustering of Applications with Noise)

DBSCAN is a density-based clustering algorithm that can identify clusters of varying shapes and sizes. It works well with noise and outliers.

How DBSCAN Works:

1. **Density-Based Clustering**: Groups data points that are closely packed together while marking points in low-density regions as outliers.
2. **Parameters**: Requires two parameters – the maximum distance between two samples for one to be considered as in the neighborhood (ε) and the minimum number of points required to form a dense region (min_samples).

Advantages:

- **Handles Noise**: Effectively deals with noise and outliers.
- **Flexible Shape**: Can find clusters of arbitrary shapes.

Limitations:

- **Parameter Sensitivity**: Performance can be sensitive to the choice of ε and min_samples.
- **Scalability**: May become less effective with very large datasets.

Implementing DBSCAN with Scikit-Learn:

```
from sklearn.cluster import DBSCAN

# Initialize DBSCAN with ε and min_samples
dbscan = DBSCAN(eps=0.5, min_samples=5)
```

```
# Fit the model to the data
clusters = dbscan.fit_predict(X)
```

Dimensionality Reduction: Simplifying Complex Data

Dimensionality reduction techniques aim to reduce the number of features in a dataset while preserving as much information as possible. This can help in visualizing high-dimensional data and improving the performance of machine learning models.

Principal Component Analysis (PCA)

PCA is a widely used technique for dimensionality reduction that transforms the data into a new coordinate system, with the axes (principal components) ordered by the amount of variance they capture.

How PCA Works:

1. **Standardization**: Standardize the data to have zero mean and unit variance.
2. **Covariance Matrix**: Compute the covariance matrix to understand the relationships between features.
3. **Eigen Decomposition**: Perform eigen decomposition to find the principal components (eigenvectors) and their corresponding eigenvalues.
4. **Projection**: Project the data onto the top principal components to reduce dimensionality.

Advantages:

- **Variance Maximization**: PCA captures the most variance in the data with the fewest number of components.
- **Visualization**: Useful for visualizing high-dimensional data in 2 or 3 dimensions.

Limitations:

- **Linearity Assumption**: PCA assumes linear relationships between features.
- **Interpretability**: Principal components may not always be easily interpretable.

Implementing PCA with Scikit-Learn:

```
from sklearn.decomposition import PCA

# Initialize PCA to reduce to 2 components
pca = PCA(n_components=2)

# Fit and transform the data
X_reduced = pca.fit_transform(X)
```

t-Distributed Stochastic Neighbor Embedding (t-SNE)

t-SNE is a technique designed for dimensionality reduction that is particularly effective for visualizing high-dimensional data. It preserves the local structure of the data while mapping it to a lower-dimensional space.

How t-SNE Works:

1. **Pairwise Similarities**: Compute pairwise similarities between data points in the high-dimensional space.
2. **Low-Dimensional Mapping**: Map the data to a lower-dimensional space while preserving the pairwise similarities.
3. **Optimization**: Use optimization techniques to minimize the divergence between the pairwise similarities in the high-dimensional and low-dimensional spaces.

Advantages:

- **Effective Visualization**: t-SNE is excellent for visualizing complex data structures and clusters.
- **Preservation of Local Structure**: Preserves local relationships and similarities.

Limitations:

- **Computationally Intensive**: t-SNE can be computationally expensive and slow for very large datasets.
- **Parameter Sensitivity**: Results can be sensitive to hyperparameters such as perplexity.

Implementing t-SNE with Scikit-Learn:

```
from sklearn.manifold import TSNE
```

```
# Initialize t-SNE
tsne = TSNE(n_components=2, perplexity=30)

# Fit and transform the data
X_reduced = tsne.fit_transform(X)
```

Unsupervised learning techniques such as clustering and dimensionality reduction are fundamental for exploring and understanding data without predefined labels. Clustering methods like K-Means, hierarchical clustering, and DBSCAN help identify natural groupings and patterns in the data, while dimensionality reduction techniques like PCA and t-SNE facilitate the simplification and visualization of complex datasets. Mastering these techniques with Scikit-Learn will empower you to uncover valuable insights and effectively manage high-dimensional data.

Chapter 11

Handling Imbalanced Datasets

Imbalanced datasets pose significant challenges in machine learning, particularly when dealing with classification problems where the classes are not represented equally. This imbalance can lead to biased models that perform well on the majority class but poorly on the minority class. This chapter explores techniques for handling imbalanced datasets, focusing on methods such as SMOTE (Synthetic Minority Over-sampling Technique) and undersampling, and their implementation using Scikit-Learn.

Understanding Imbalanced Datasets

Imbalanced datasets occur when one class significantly outnumbers the other(s). For example, in a fraud detection system, fraudulent transactions (minority class) might constitute a very small percentage of the total transactions (majority class). In such scenarios, standard classification algorithms might be biased towards the majority class, resulting in poor performance on the minority class.

Challenges with Imbalanced Datasets:

1. **Model Bias**: Standard models tend to predict the majority class more frequently, leading to misleading accuracy metrics.

2. **Poor Performance Metrics**: Metrics such as accuracy can be deceptive when dealing with imbalanced data. For instance, a model that predicts only the majority class can still achieve high accuracy if the majority class constitutes a large percentage of the dataset.

Evaluation Metrics for Imbalanced Data:

To better assess model performance on imbalanced datasets, consider using metrics such as precision, recall, F1-score, and the area under the Receiver Operating Characteristic (ROC) curve. These metrics provide a clearer picture of how well the model is performing on the minority class.

Techniques for Handling Imbalanced Datasets

1. Synthetic Minority Over-sampling Technique (SMOTE)

SMOTE is a widely used technique for addressing class imbalance by generating synthetic examples of the minority class. Instead of duplicating existing minority class samples, SMOTE creates new instances by interpolating between existing examples.

How SMOTE Works:

1. **Neighbor Selection**: For each minority class sample, identify its k-nearest neighbors.

2. **Synthetic Sample Generation**: Generate synthetic samples by randomly selecting points along the line segments between the sample and its neighbors.
3. **Augmentation**: Add these synthetic samples to the training set, effectively increasing the representation of the minority class.

Advantages of SMOTE:

- **Improves Model Training**: Provides the model with more diverse examples of the minority class, leading to better learning.
- **Reduces Overfitting**: Synthetic samples can help the model generalize better compared to duplicating existing examples.

Limitations of SMOTE:

- **Risk of Overfitting**: If not managed carefully, synthetic samples can lead to overfitting, especially if they are not diverse enough.
- **Increased Computational Cost**: Generating synthetic samples adds to the computational complexity.

Implementing SMOTE with Scikit-Learn:

```
from imblearn.over_sampling import SMOTE

# Initialize SMOTE with the desired ratio
smote = SMOTE(sampling_strategy='minority')
```

```
# Fit and transform the data
X_resampled, y_resampled = smote.fit_resample(X, y)
```

2. Undersampling

Undersampling involves reducing the number of instances in the majority class to balance the class distribution. This technique can be useful when dealing with very large datasets where the majority class is overwhelmingly represented.

How Undersampling Works:

1. **Random Sampling**: Randomly select a subset of the majority class instances to match the number of instances in the minority class.
2. **Dataset Reduction**: Create a balanced dataset by combining the undersampled majority class with the original minority class.

Advantages of Undersampling:

- **Simpler and Faster**: Reduces the size of the dataset, making it easier and faster to train models.
- **Reduces Imbalance**: Balances the class distribution without adding synthetic samples.

Limitations of Undersampling:

- **Loss of Information**: Reducing the majority class can lead to the loss of potentially valuable data.

- **Potential Underfitting**: The model may underperform if too many majority class instances are removed.

Implementing Undersampling with Scikit-Learn:

```
from imblearn.under_sampling import RandomUnderSampler

# Initialize RandomUnderSampler
under_sampler = RandomUnderSampler(sampling_strategy='minority')

# Fit and transform the data
X_resampled, y_resampled = under_sampler.fit_resample(X, y)
```

Advanced Techniques

3. Combination of Over-Sampling and Under-Sampling

Combining SMOTE and undersampling methods can be an effective strategy for handling imbalanced datasets. This approach, known as SMOTEENN (SMOTE + Edited Nearest Neighbors), generates synthetic samples for the minority class while also removing noisy or redundant samples from the majority class.

How SMOTEENN Works:

1. **Apply SMOTE**: Generate synthetic samples for the minority class.

2. **Apply Edited Nearest Neighbors**: Clean up the majority class by removing noisy samples.
3. **Combine**: Create a balanced dataset using the combined approach.

Implementing SMOTEENN with Scikit-Learn:

from imblearn.combine import SMOTEENN

# Initialize SMOTEENN
smote_enn = SMOTEENN()

Fit and transform the data
X_resampled,   y_resampled   =
smote_enn.fit_resample(X, y)

4. Cost-Sensitive Learning

Cost-sensitive learning involves adjusting the learning algorithm to penalize misclassifications of the minority class more heavily. This approach can be useful when modifying the data distribution is not feasible.

How Cost-Sensitive Learning Works:

1. **Define Costs**: Specify different costs for misclassifications of each class.
2. **Incorporate Costs**: Integrate these costs into the training process to bias the model towards the minority class.

Implementing Cost-Sensitive Learning with Scikit-Learn:

```
from sklearn.ensemble import RandomForestClassifier

# Initialize RandomForestClassifier with class weights
classifier                                          =
RandomForestClassifier(class_weight='balanced')

# Fit the model
classifier.fit(X, y)
```

Best Practices for Handling Imbalanced Datasets

1. **Evaluate Multiple Metrics**: Use a variety of metrics (e.g., precision, recall, F1-score) to evaluate model performance comprehensively.
2. **Cross-Validation**: Employ cross-validation to ensure that the model generalizes well across different subsets of the data.
3. **Experiment with Different Techniques**: Test various sampling methods and combinations to find the most effective approach for your specific dataset.
4. **Monitor Model Performance**: Continuously monitor the model's performance on both the majority and minority classes to ensure balanced accuracy.

Handling imbalanced datasets is crucial for building robust machine learning models that perform well across all classes. Techniques such as SMOTE and undersampling offer effective ways to address class imbalance, each with its advantages and limitations. By applying these methods and best practices, you can improve the performance of your models and achieve more equitable results across different classes.

Chapter 12

Cross-Validation and Model Selection

Cross-validation is a critical technique in machine learning that helps assess how well a model generalizes to unseen data. It provides a robust method for evaluating model performance and selecting the most suitable model for a given problem. This chapter will explore various cross-validation techniques, discuss how to split datasets effectively, and utilize Scikit-Learn's tools for implementing k-fold cross-validation and model selection.

Understanding Cross-Validation

Cross-validation is a technique used to evaluate the performance of a model by dividing the dataset into multiple subsets or folds. The model is trained on some of these subsets and tested on the remaining ones. This process helps ensure that the model performs well across different segments of the data and is not overfitting to a specific training set.

Why Cross-Validation Matters

1. **Assess Model Generalization**: Cross-validation provides insights into how a model will perform on unseen data, helping to gauge its ability to generalize.

2. **Prevent Overfitting**: By evaluating the model on different subsets of data, cross-validation helps to identify and mitigate overfitting issues.
3. **Optimize Model Selection**: It allows for a fair comparison between different models or hyperparameter settings, guiding the selection of the best-performing model.

Dataset Splitting Techniques

Properly splitting the dataset is essential for effective cross-validation. There are several techniques for splitting data, each with its advantages and use cases.

Train-Test Split

The simplest approach involves splitting the dataset into two parts: a training set and a test set.

How It Works:

1. **Split the Data**: Divide the dataset into a training set (used to train the model) and a test set (used to evaluate the model).
2. **Train and Evaluate**: Train the model on the training set and evaluate its performance on the test set.

Advantages:

- **Simplicity**: Easy to implement and understand.

- **Quick Evaluation**: Provides a straightforward measure of model performance.

Limitations:

- **Single Evaluation**: Only one train-test split is used, which may not capture the variability in the data.

Implementing Train-Test Split with Scikit-Learn:

```
from sklearn.model_selection import train_test_split

# Split the data into training and test sets
X_train, X_test, y_train, y_test = train_test_split(X, y, test_size=0.2, random_state=42)
```

k-Fold Cross-Validation

k-Fold Cross-Validation is a more comprehensive technique that divides the dataset into k folds. The model is trained k times, each time using a different fold as the test set and the remaining k-1 folds as the training set.

How It Works:

1. **Divide the Data**: Split the dataset into k equally sized folds.
2. **Train and Test**: Train the model on k-1 folds and test it on the remaining fold.
3. **Repeat**: Repeat the process k times, using each fold as the test set once.

4. **Aggregate Results**: Average the performance metrics across all k iterations to obtain a final performance estimate.

Advantages:

- **Comprehensive Evaluation**: Provides a more robust measure of model performance by using multiple train-test splits.
- **Efficient Use of Data**: Utilizes all data points for both training and testing.

Limitations:

- **Computationally Intensive**: Can be time-consuming and computationally expensive, especially with large datasets and complex models.

Implementing k-Fold Cross-Validation with Scikit-Learn:

```
from sklearn.model_selection import cross_val_score

# Perform k-Fold Cross-Validation
scores = cross_val_score(model, X, y, cv=5)
```

Stratified k-Fold Cross-Validation

Stratified k-Fold Cross-Validation is a variant of k-Fold that ensures each fold has the same proportion of classes as the entire dataset. This is particularly useful for imbalanced datasets.

How It Works:

1. **Stratify the Data**: Divide the dataset into k folds, maintaining the proportion of each class in each fold.
2. **Train and Test**: Similar to k-Fold Cross-Validation, but with stratification to handle imbalanced classes.

Advantages:

- **Balanced Folds**: Ensures that each fold is representative of the class distribution.
- **Improved Performance Estimates**: Provides more reliable estimates of model performance on imbalanced datasets.

Implementing Stratified k-Fold Cross-Validation with Scikit-Learn:

```
from sklearn.model_selection import StratifiedKFold

# Initialize StratifiedKFold
skf = StratifiedKFold(n_splits=5)

# Perform Stratified k-Fold Cross-Validation
for train_index, test_index in skf.split(X, y):
    X_train, X_test = X[train_index], X[test_index]
    y_train, y_test = y[train_index], y[test_index]
    # Train and evaluate the model
```

Model Selection and Hyperparameter Tuning

Selecting the best model and tuning its hyperparameters is crucial for achieving optimal performance. Scikit-Learn provides several tools to facilitate this process.

Grid Search

Grid Search is a technique used to perform an exhaustive search over a specified hyperparameter grid. It evaluates all possible combinations of hyperparameters to find the best-performing model.

How It Works:

1. **Define the Hyperparameter Grid**: Specify the range of values for each hyperparameter.
2. **Evaluate Combinations**: Train and evaluate the model for all possible combinations of hyperparameters using cross-validation.
3. **Select the Best Combination**: Choose the combination that yields the best performance.

Advantages:

- **Comprehensive Search**: Evaluates all possible hyperparameter combinations.
- **Systematic Approach**: Provides a structured method for hyperparameter tuning.

Limitations:

- **Computationally Expensive**: Can be time-consuming, especially with a large number of hyperparameters or values.

Implementing Grid Search with Scikit-Learn:

```
from sklearn.model_selection import GridSearchCV

# Define the hyperparameter grid
param_grid = {'n_estimators': [50, 100], 'max_depth':
[10, 20]}

# Initialize GridSearchCV
grid_search    =    GridSearchCV(estimator=model,
param_grid=param_grid, cv=5)

# Fit GridSearchCV
grid_search.fit(X, y)

# Best parameters
best_params = grid_search.best_params_
```

Random Search

Random Search is an alternative to Grid Search that samples random combinations of hyperparameters. It is often more efficient and can explore a broader range of hyperparameters.

How It Works:

1. **Define the Hyperparameter Space**: Specify ranges or distributions for each hyperparameter.
2. **Sample Random Combinations**: Randomly sample combinations of hyperparameters and evaluate them using cross-validation.
3. **Select the Best Combination**: Choose the combination that performs best according to the evaluation metrics.

Advantages:

- **Less Computationally Intensive**: Requires fewer evaluations compared to Grid Search.
- **Broader Exploration**: Can explore a wider range of hyperparameters.

Limitations:

- **Less Systematic**: May not cover all possible hyperparameter combinations.

Implementing Random Search with Scikit-Learn:

```
from        sklearn.model_selection        import
RandomizedSearchCV

# Define the hyperparameter space
param_distributions  =  {'n_estimators':  [50,  100],
'max_depth': [10, 20]}

# Initialize RandomizedSearchCV
```

```
random_search                                    =
RandomizedSearchCV(estimator=model,
param_distributions=param_distributions,   n_iter=10,
cv=5)

# Fit RandomizedSearchCV
random_search.fit(X, y)

# Best parameters
best_params = random_search.best_params_
```

Model Evaluation and Selection

After performing cross-validation and hyperparameter tuning, evaluate the model's performance using various metrics and select the best model based on these evaluations.

Key Evaluation Metrics:

- **Accuracy**: Measures the proportion of correctly classified instances.
- **Precision**: Indicates the proportion of true positives among the predicted positives.
- **Recall**: Measures the proportion of true positives among the actual positives.
- **F1-Score**: Combines precision and recall into a single metric.

Implementing Model Evaluation with Scikit-Learn:

```
from sklearn.metrics import classification_report

# Predict on the test set
y_pred = model.predict(X_test)

# Print classification report
print(classification_report(y_test, y_pred))
```

Best Practices for Model Selection

1. **Use Cross-Validation**: Always validate models using cross-validation to ensure they generalize well.
2. **Explore Multiple Models**: Test different models and hyperparameters to find the best-performing combination.
3. **Monitor Overfitting**: Watch for signs of overfitting and use techniques like regularization if needed.
4. **Evaluate Thoroughly**: Use a variety of metrics to assess model performance comprehensively.

Cross-validation and model selection are crucial for developing robust machine learning models. By understanding and applying techniques such as k-Fold Cross-Validation, Grid Search, and Random Search, you can ensure that your models are well-tuned and perform optimally on unseen data. Scikit-Learn offers powerful tools to facilitate these processes, helping you achieve high-performing and reliable models.

Chapter 13

Hyperparameter Tuning with Grid Search and Random Search

Hyperparameter tuning is an essential step in the machine learning pipeline, allowing you to optimize your model's performance by finding the most suitable parameters. Effective tuning can significantly improve a model's accuracy, efficiency, and overall effectiveness. This chapter delves into the concepts of hyperparameter tuning and provides a detailed guide on using Scikit-Learn's GridSearchCV and RandomizedSearchCV for this purpose.

Understanding Hyperparameters

Hyperparameters are parameters set before the learning process begins and are not learned from the data. They control various aspects of the model's training process and structure, such as the depth of a decision tree or the number of neighbors in a K-nearest neighbors (KNN) model. Unlike model parameters, which are learned from the data, hyperparameters need to be manually set and tuned to achieve optimal performance.

Types of Hyperparameters

1. **Model-Specific Hyperparameters**: These include parameters like the number of trees in a random forest,

the kernel type in a Support Vector Machine (SVM), or the learning rate in gradient boosting.

2. **Training Hyperparameters**: These are related to the training process, such as the number of epochs, batch size, and learning rate.

Grid Search for Hyperparameter Tuning

Grid Search is a systematic approach to hyperparameter tuning that involves specifying a grid of hyperparameter values and evaluating the model's performance for each combination. This technique ensures that all possible combinations are explored to find the best set of parameters.

How Grid Search Works

1. **Define the Hyperparameter Grid**: Specify a range or list of values for each hyperparameter you want to tune.
2. **Train and Evaluate**: For each combination of hyperparameters, train the model and evaluate its performance using cross-validation.
3. **Select the Best Combination**: Choose the hyperparameter combination that yields the highest performance based on a chosen metric.

Advantages:

- **Comprehensive Search**: Evaluates all possible combinations within the defined grid.

- **Systematic Approach**: Provides a structured method for finding the best hyperparameters.

Limitations:

- **Computationally Expensive**: Can be time-consuming, especially with a large number of hyperparameters or values.
- **Grid Size Limitation**: Limited to the predefined grid, potentially missing optimal values outside the grid.

Implementing Grid Search with Scikit-Learn

Scikit-Learn's GridSearchCV class facilitates Grid Search by automating the process of training and evaluating models with different hyperparameters.

Example Implementation:

```python
from sklearn.model_selection import GridSearchCV
from sklearn.ensemble import RandomForestClassifier

# Define the hyperparameter grid
param_grid = {
    'n_estimators': [50, 100, 200],
    'max_depth': [10, 20, 30],
    'min_samples_split': [2, 5, 10]
}

# Initialize the model
model = RandomForestClassifier()
```

```
# Initialize GridSearchCV
grid_search    =    GridSearchCV(estimator=model,
param_grid=param_grid, cv=5, n_jobs=-1)

# Fit GridSearchCV
grid_search.fit(X_train, y_train)

# Get the best parameters
best_params = grid_search.best_params_
print("Best parameters found: ", best_params)

# Best model
best_model = grid_search.best_estimator_
```

Random Search for Hyperparameter Tuning

Random Search is an alternative to Grid Search that samples random combinations of hyperparameters rather than evaluating all possible combinations. This approach can be more efficient, especially when dealing with large hyperparameter spaces.

How Random Search Works

1. **Define the Hyperparameter Space**: Specify ranges or distributions for each hyperparameter.
2. **Sample Random Combinations**: Randomly sample a specified number of hyperparameter combinations.

3. **Train and Evaluate**: Train and evaluate the model for each sampled combination using cross-validation.
4. **Select the Best Combination**: Choose the combination that performs best based on the evaluation metric.

Advantages:

- **Less Computationally Intensive**: Requires fewer evaluations compared to Grid Search.
- **Broader Exploration**: Can explore a wider range of hyperparameters.

Limitations:

- **Less Comprehensive**: May miss the optimal hyperparameter values not sampled.
- **Stochastic Nature**: Results can vary between different runs.

Implementing Random Search with Scikit-Learn

Scikit-Learn's RandomizedSearchCV class automates Random Search, allowing you to specify a distribution or list of hyperparameter values and sample randomly.

Example Implementation:

```
from         sklearn.model_selection         import
RandomizedSearchCV
from         sklearn.ensemble         import
GradientBoostingClassifier
```

```python
from scipy.stats import randint

# Define the hyperparameter space
param_distributions = {
    'n_estimators': randint(50, 200),
    'learning_rate': [0.01, 0.1, 0.2],
    'max_depth': randint(3, 10)
}

# Initialize the model
model = GradientBoostingClassifier()

# Initialize RandomizedSearchCV
random_search = RandomizedSearchCV(estimator=model,
param_distributions=param_distributions,    n_iter=10,
cv=5, n_jobs=-1, random_state=42)

# Fit RandomizedSearchCV
random_search.fit(X_train, y_train)

# Get the best parameters
best_params = random_search.best_params_
print("Best parameters found: ", best_params)

# Best model
best_model = random_search.best_estimator_
```

Comparing Grid Search and Random Search

Both Grid Search and Random Search have their own strengths and are suitable for different scenarios:

- **Grid Search**: Best for smaller hyperparameter spaces where a comprehensive search is feasible.
- **Random Search**: Better for larger hyperparameter spaces or when computational resources are limited, as it can explore a broader range more efficiently.

Best Practices for Hyperparameter Tuning

1. **Define a Reasonable Grid/Space**: Ensure that the hyperparameter grid or space is large enough to explore potential solutions but manageable to avoid excessive computation.
2. **Use Cross-Validation**: Always validate models using cross-validation to get a reliable estimate of performance.
3. **Monitor Overfitting**: Be aware of overfitting when tuning hyperparameters, especially if using a small dataset.
4. **Evaluate Multiple Metrics**: Consider multiple evaluation metrics to get a comprehensive view of model performance.

Hyperparameter tuning is a critical aspect of optimizing machine learning models. By mastering Grid Search and Random Search techniques, you can effectively fine-tune your models to achieve the best possible performance. Scikit-Learn's tools provide powerful and flexible methods for exploring hyperparameter spaces, helping you build high-impact machine learning models with Pythonic precision.

Chapter 14

Feature Selection and Importance

Feature selection is a crucial step in the machine learning pipeline, impacting model performance, interpretability, and computational efficiency. By focusing on the most relevant features, you can enhance model accuracy, reduce overfitting, and streamline the training process. This chapter explores various techniques for selecting and assessing feature importance, leveraging Scikit-Learn's powerful tools.

Understanding Feature Selection

Feature selection involves choosing a subset of the most important features from the dataset, thereby improving model performance and reducing complexity. This process is essential for several reasons:

1. **Improves Model Accuracy**: By removing irrelevant or redundant features, you can improve the model's ability to generalize to unseen data.
2. **Reduces Overfitting**: Fewer features reduce the risk of the model fitting noise or irrelevant patterns in the training data.
3. **Enhances Model Interpretability**: A model with fewer features is easier to interpret and understand.

4. **Decreases Computational Cost**: Fewer features result in faster training times and reduced computational resource requirements.

Techniques for Feature Selection

Filter Methods

Filter methods assess the relevance of features based on statistical measures. These methods are independent of the model and are often used as a preprocessing step.

Examples of Filter Methods:

- **Correlation Coefficient**: Measures the linear relationship between features and the target variable. Features with low correlation to the target may be removed.
- **Chi-Square Test**: Evaluates the independence of categorical features with respect to the target variable. Features with high chi-square scores are considered more relevant.

Wrapper Methods

Wrapper methods evaluate feature subsets based on the model's performance. They are computationally expensive but can provide better results as they consider feature interactions.

Examples of Wrapper Methods:

- **Recursive Feature Elimination (RFE)**: Iteratively builds models and eliminates the least important features based on model performance.

Advantages:

- **Model-Specific**: Tailored to the performance of a specific model, which can lead to more accurate feature selection.
- **Considers Feature Interactions**: Evaluates feature subsets based on how they interact with the model.

Limitations:

- **Computationally Intensive**: Requires training multiple models, which can be time-consuming.
- **Risk of Overfitting**: Particularly if the feature space is large and the dataset is small.

Embedded Methods

Embedded methods perform feature selection as part of the model training process. They combine aspects of both filter and wrapper methods.

Examples of Embedded Methods:

- **Lasso Regression**: Adds an L1 penalty to the regression model, which can shrink some feature coefficients to zero, effectively performing feature selection.

- **Tree-Based Methods**: Algorithms like Random Forests and Gradient Boosting provide feature importance scores based on the contribution of each feature to the model's predictions.

Using Scikit-Learn for Feature Selection

Scikit-Learn offers several tools for implementing feature selection techniques effectively. This section explores key methods, including Recursive Feature Elimination (RFE) and feature importance scores from tree-based models.

Recursive Feature Elimination (RFE)

RFE is a wrapper method that recursively removes the least important features based on model performance. It involves the following steps:

1. **Train the Model**: Fit the model using all available features.
2. **Rank Features**: Assess feature importance based on model weights or performance metrics.
3. **Eliminate Features**: Remove the least important features.
4. **Repeat**: Continue the process until the desired number of features is reached.

Implementation with Scikit-Learn:

```
from sklearn.feature_selection import RFE
```

```python
from sklearn.linear_model import LogisticRegression

# Initialize the model
model = LogisticRegression()

# Initialize RFE
selector          =          RFE(estimator=model,
n_features_to_select=5)

# Fit RFE
selector = selector.fit(X_train, y_train)

# Get the selected features
selected_features = selector.support_
print("Selected features: ", selected_features)
```

Feature Importance from Tree-Based Models

Tree-based models, such as Random Forests and Gradient Boosting, provide feature importance scores based on how features contribute to reducing impurity in decision trees. These scores can be used to identify the most important features.

Implementation with Scikit-Learn:

```python
from sklearn.ensemble import RandomForestClassifier

# Initialize the model
model = RandomForestClassifier()
```

143

```
# Train the model
model.fit(X_train, y_train)

# Get feature importance scores
importances = model.feature_importances_
indices = np.argsort(importances)[::-1]

# Print feature importance
for i in indices:
    print(f"Feature {i}: {importances[i]}")
```

Feature Selection Best Practices

1. **Start with Domain Knowledge**: Utilize domain expertise to select initial features before applying automated methods.
2. **Use Multiple Methods**: Combine different feature selection techniques to ensure robustness.
3. **Validate Selected Features**: Ensure that the selected features improve model performance and do not lead to overfitting.
4. **Consider Feature Interactions**: Be mindful of interactions between features that might impact model performance.

Feature selection is a fundamental aspect of building effective machine learning models. By using Scikit-Learn's tools like Recursive Feature Elimination and feature importance scores, you can systematically identify and select the most impactful features. This not only improves model performance but also enhances interpretability and reduces computational costs. Employing a combination of feature selection techniques ensures that your models are both accurate and efficient.

Chapter 15

Handling Categorical Data and Encoding Techniques

Categorical data is a common type of data encountered in machine learning tasks, and properly handling it is essential for building effective models. Unlike numerical data, categorical data represents discrete values that can be non-numeric, such as labels or categories. This chapter explores various methods for encoding categorical features, focusing on techniques like one-hot encoding, label encoding, and ordinal encoding, and demonstrates their implementation using Scikit-Learn's preprocessing tools.

Understanding Categorical Data

Categorical data can be classified into two main types:

1. **Nominal Data**: Categories that have no inherent order or ranking. Examples include colors (red, blue, green) or types of animals (cat, dog, bird).
2. **Ordinal Data**: Categories with a meaningful order or ranking but without fixed intervals between categories. Examples include education levels (high school, bachelor's, master's) or satisfaction ratings (low, medium, high).

Proper encoding of categorical data is crucial because most machine learning algorithms require numerical

146

input. Encoding techniques convert categorical values into a format that algorithms can process effectively.

Encoding Techniques

One-Hot Encoding

One-hot encoding is a popular method for converting categorical variables into a binary matrix. Each category is represented by a binary vector, where only one element is 1 (indicating the presence of that category) and all other elements are 0.

Advantages:

- **No Ordinal Assumptions**: Suitable for nominal data where no ordinal relationship exists.
- **Simple and Effective**: Easy to implement and understand.

Limitations:

- **Increased Dimensionality**: Can lead to a large number of features, especially with high cardinality.

Implementation with Scikit-Learn:

```
from sklearn.preprocessing import OneHotEncoder
import pandas as pd

# Sample data
```

```python
data = pd.DataFrame({'Color': ['Red', 'Blue', 'Green',
'Red']})

# Initialize OneHotEncoder
encoder = OneHotEncoder(sparse=False)

# Fit and transform the data
encoded_data = encoder.fit_transform(data[['Color']])
encoded_df       =       pd.DataFrame(encoded_data,
columns=encoder.get_feature_names_out(['Color']))

print("One-Hot Encoded Data:")
print(encoded_df)
```

Label Encoding

Label encoding converts each category into a unique integer. This method is straightforward but introduces an ordinal relationship between categories, which may not be appropriate for nominal data.

Advantages:

- **Simple and Compact**: Suitable for algorithms that can handle categorical values directly.

Limitations:

- **Ordinal Assumptions**: Implies an ordinal relationship between categories, which may lead to misleading results for nominal data.

Implementation with Scikit-Learn:

```
from sklearn.preprocessing import LabelEncoder
import pandas as pd

# Sample data
data = pd.DataFrame({'Color': ['Red', 'Blue', 'Green',
'Red']})

# Initialize LabelEncoder
encoder = LabelEncoder()

# Fit and transform the data
data['Color_Encoded']                            =
encoder.fit_transform(data['Color'])

print("Label Encoded Data:")
print(data)
```

Ordinal Encoding

Ordinal encoding is used for data with a meaningful order. Each category is assigned an integer value that reflects its rank or order.

Advantages:

- **Reflects Order**: Suitable for ordinal data where order matters.

Limitations:

- **Limited to Ordinal Data**: Not appropriate for nominal data where no inherent order exists.

Implementation with Scikit-Learn:

```python
from sklearn.preprocessing import OrdinalEncoder
import pandas as pd

# Sample data
data = pd.DataFrame({'Education': ['High School', 'Bachelor', 'Master', 'PhD']})

# Define the order
categories = [['High School', 'Bachelor', 'Master', 'PhD']]

# Initialize OrdinalEncoder
encoder = OrdinalEncoder(categories=categories)

# Fit and transform the data
encoded_data = encoder.fit_transform(data[['Education']])
data['Education_Encoded'] = encoded_data

print("Ordinal Encoded Data:")
print(data)
```

Choosing the Right Encoding Technique

Selecting the appropriate encoding technique depends on the type of categorical data:

1. **Nominal Data**: Use one-hot encoding to avoid introducing unintended ordinal relationships.
2. **Ordinal Data**: Use ordinal encoding to preserve the inherent order of categories.

Combining Encoding with Other Preprocessing Steps

Often, categorical encoding is combined with other preprocessing steps, such as:

- **Scaling**: Normalizing numerical features after encoding categorical variables.
- **Feature Engineering**: Creating new features or combining existing ones to improve model performance.

Example of Combining One-Hot Encoding with Feature Scaling:

```python
from sklearn.preprocessing import StandardScaler
from sklearn.compose import ColumnTransformer
from sklearn.pipeline import Pipeline

# Sample data with both categorical and numerical features
data = pd.DataFrame({
    'Color': ['Red', 'Blue', 'Green', 'Red'],
```

```python
    'Price': [20000, 25000, 30000, 22000]
})

# Define the preprocessing steps
preprocessor = ColumnTransformer(
    transformers=[
        ('color', OneHotEncoder(), ['Color']),
        ('price', StandardScaler(), ['Price'])
    ])

# Apply preprocessing
processed_data = preprocessor.fit_transform(data)
processed_df = pd.DataFrame(processed_data,
columns=['Color_Blue', 'Color_Green', 'Color_Red',
'Price'])

print("Processed Data:")
print(processed_df)
```

Handling categorical data and applying the correct encoding techniques is essential for building effective machine learning models. Scikit-Learn provides robust tools for implementing one-hot encoding, label encoding, and ordinal encoding, enabling you to prepare categorical features for various algorithms. By understanding and applying these techniques, you can ensure that your models receive properly formatted input, leading to improved performance and more accurate predictions.

Chapter 16

Principal Component Analysis (PCA) and Other Dimensionality Reduction Techniques

Dimensionality reduction is a vital aspect of data preprocessing, particularly when dealing with high-dimensional datasets. It helps in simplifying models, reducing computational costs, and uncovering patterns by transforming features into a lower-dimensional space. This chapter delves into Principal Component Analysis (PCA) and explores other dimensionality reduction techniques such as Linear Discriminant Analysis (LDA), illustrating their applications using Scikit-Learn.

Understanding Dimensionality Reduction

Dimensionality reduction techniques are used to reduce the number of features in a dataset while preserving as much information as possible. This can enhance the performance of machine learning algorithms by mitigating issues related to the curse of dimensionality, which occurs when the number of features grows excessively.

Key Benefits of Dimensionality Reduction:

- **Improved Performance**: Reducing the number of features can lead to faster training times and more efficient models.

- **Reduced Overfitting**: Simplified models are less likely to overfit the training data.
- **Enhanced Visualization**: Lower-dimensional data can be visualized more easily, providing insights into the structure and relationships within the data.
- **Data Compression**: Dimensionality reduction techniques can compress data, making it more manageable and easier to store.

Principal Component Analysis (PCA)

PCA is one of the most widely used dimensionality reduction techniques. It transforms data into a new coordinate system where the greatest variance by any projection of the data comes to lie on the first coordinate (the first principal component), the second greatest variance on the second coordinate, and so on.

How PCA Works

1. **Standardize the Data**: PCA requires the data to be centered and scaled. Standardization ensures that each feature contributes equally to the analysis.
2. **Compute the Covariance Matrix**: The covariance matrix captures the relationships between features.
3. **Calculate Eigenvalues and Eigenvectors**: Eigenvalues represent the magnitude of variance captured by each principal component, and eigenvectors represent the directions of these components.

4. **Select Principal Components**: Choose the top principal components based on the largest eigenvalues to retain the most variance.
5. **Transform the Data**: Project the original data onto the selected principal components to obtain the reduced dataset.

Implementation with Scikit-Learn

```
from sklearn.decomposition import PCA
from sklearn.preprocessing import StandardScaler
import pandas as pd

# Sample data
data = pd.DataFrame({
    'Feature1': [2.5, 3.5, 4.5, 5.5],
    'Feature2': [3.0, 4.0, 2.0, 5.0]
})

# Standardize the data
scaler = StandardScaler()
scaled_data = scaler.fit_transform(data)

# Initialize PCA
pca = PCA(n_components=1)  # Reduce to 1 principal component

# Fit and transform the data
pca_data = pca.fit_transform(scaled_data)
```

```
# Convert to DataFrame for better readability
pca_df = pd.DataFrame(pca_data, columns=['Principal
Component 1'])

print("PCA Transformed Data:")
print(pca_df)
```

Linear Discriminant Analysis (LDA)

LDA is another powerful technique for dimensionality
reduction, particularly suited for classification
problems. Unlike PCA, which is unsupervised, LDA is
supervised and focuses on finding the components that
best separate different classes.

How LDA Works

1. **Compute the Within-Class and Between-Class
   Scatter Matrices**: These matrices capture the variance
   within each class and between different classes.
2. **Calculate Eigenvalues and Eigenvectors**:
   Eigenvalues represent the discriminatory power of
   each component, while eigenvectors define the
   directions of these components.
3. **Select Discriminant Components**: Choose the top
   components that maximize the separation between
   classes.
4. **Transform the Data**: Project the data onto the
   selected discriminant components to achieve
   dimensionality reduction.

Implementation with Scikit-Learn

```python
from sklearn.discriminant_analysis import LinearDiscriminantAnalysis
from sklearn.preprocessing import StandardScaler
import pandas as pd
import numpy as np

# Sample data
X = np.array([[1, 2], [3, 4], [5, 6], [7, 8]])
y = np.array([0, 0, 1, 1])  # Binary class labels

# Standardize the data
scaler = StandardScaler()
X_scaled = scaler.fit_transform(X)

# Initialize LDA
lda = LinearDiscriminantAnalysis(n_components=1)  # Reduce to 1 discriminant component

# Fit and transform the data
lda_data = lda.fit_transform(X_scaled, y)

# Convert to DataFrame for better readability
lda_df = pd.DataFrame(lda_data, columns=['Discriminant Component 1'])

print("LDA Transformed Data:")
print(lda_df)
```

Other Dimensionality Reduction Techniques

t-Distributed Stochastic Neighbor Embedding (t-SNE)

t-SNE is a technique particularly useful for visualizing high-dimensional data in two or three dimensions. It emphasizes preserving the local structure of data, making it ideal for exploring clusters and patterns.

Implementation with Scikit-Learn:

```python
from sklearn.manifold import TSNE
import pandas as pd

# Sample data
data = pd.DataFrame({
    'Feature1': [2.5, 3.5, 4.5, 5.5],
    'Feature2': [3.0, 4.0, 2.0, 5.0]
})

# Initialize t-SNE
tsne = TSNE(n_components=2, random_state=0)

# Fit and transform the data
tsne_data = tsne.fit_transform(data)

# Convert to DataFrame for better readability
tsne_df        =        pd.DataFrame(tsne_data,
columns=['Dimension 1', 'Dimension 2'])
```

```
print("t-SNE Transformed Data:")
print(tsne_df)
```

Independent Component Analysis (ICA)

ICA is used to separate a multivariate signal into additive, independent components. It is often used in signal processing and blind source separation.

Implementation with Scikit-Learn:

```python
from sklearn.decomposition import FastICA
import pandas as pd

# Sample data
data = pd.DataFrame({
    'Feature1': [2.5, 3.5, 4.5, 5.5],
    'Feature2': [3.0, 4.0, 2.0, 5.0]
})

# Initialize ICA
ica = FastICA(n_components=2, random_state=0)

# Fit and transform the data
ica_data = ica.fit_transform(data)

# Convert to DataFrame for better readability
ica_df = pd.DataFrame(ica_data, columns=['Component 1', 'Component 2'])
```

```
print("ICA Transformed Data:")
print(ica_df)
```

Choosing the Right Dimensionality Reduction Technique

- **PCA**: Best for reducing dimensionality while preserving the most variance in the data. Suitable for unsupervised learning tasks.
- **LDA**: Ideal for supervised learning tasks where you need to enhance class separability.
- **t-SNE**: Effective for visualizing high-dimensional data in a lower-dimensional space.
- **ICA**: Useful for separating mixed signals into independent components.

Dimensionality reduction is a critical step in the machine learning pipeline, enabling the simplification of models and enhancing their performance. PCA and LDA are foundational techniques, each with its strengths and applications. By utilizing Scikit-Learn's tools for these and other dimensionality reduction techniques, you can efficiently handle high-dimensional data, uncover underlying patterns, and improve your models' effectiveness.

Chapter 17

Anomaly Detection Using Machine Learning

Anomaly detection, or outlier detection, involves identifying patterns in data that deviate significantly from the norm. This is crucial in various domains such as fraud detection, network security, and fault detection in industrial systems. This chapter explores anomaly detection techniques, focusing on models like Isolation Forests and One-Class Support Vector Machines (SVM), and demonstrates their implementation using Scikit-Learn.

Understanding Anomaly Detection

Anomaly detection aims to identify observations that do not fit the general pattern of the data. These anomalies can be indicative of critical issues, such as fraud, system malfunctions, or novel events.

Key Concepts:

- **Anomalies**: Data points that are significantly different from the majority of the data.
- **Outliers**: Points that lie outside the general distribution of the dataset, often considered anomalies.

Types of Anomaly Detection:

1. **Supervised Anomaly Detection**: Requires labeled data to train the model, where anomalies are known in advance.
2. **Unsupervised Anomaly Detection**: Does not require labeled data and identifies anomalies based on the structure of the data itself.

Isolation Forests

Isolation Forest is an ensemble-based anomaly detection method that isolates anomalies instead of profiling normal data. It works by randomly selecting features and splitting values to isolate observations. Anomalies are those that are easier to isolate compared to normal data.

How Isolation Forest Works

1. **Build Isolation Trees**: Construct multiple isolation trees by randomly selecting features and split values.
2. **Measure Path Length**: The path length from the root to the leaf of an isolation tree is used to determine the anomaly score. Shorter paths indicate anomalies.
3. **Aggregate Results**: Combine the results from multiple trees to decide whether an observation is an anomaly.

Implementation with Scikit-Learn

```
from sklearn.ensemble import IsolationForest
import numpy as np
import pandas as pd
```

```python
# Sample data
data = pd.DataFrame({
    'Feature1': [1, 2, 3, 4, 5, 100],
    'Feature2': [1, 2, 3, 4, 5, 200]
})

# Initialize Isolation Forest
iso_forest = IsolationForest(contamination=0.1,
random_state=0)

# Fit the model
iso_forest.fit(data)

# Predict anomalies
anomalies = iso_forest.predict(data)

# Convert predictions to a DataFrame
data['Anomaly'] = anomalies
data['Anomaly'] = data['Anomaly'].map({1: 'Normal', -
1: 'Anomaly'})

print("Isolation Forest Anomaly Detection:")
print(data)
```

One-Class SVM

One-Class SVM is a variant of Support Vector
Machines used for anomaly detection. It is particularly
suited for high-dimensional data and works by learning

a decision function for outlier detection. It tries to find a hyperplane that best separates the majority of the data from the origin.

How One-Class SVM Works

1. **Fit the Model**: Train the SVM model on the data to learn a decision boundary that captures the majority of the data.
2. **Predict Anomalies**: Use the decision function to classify data points as normal or anomalies based on their distance from the learned boundary.

Implementation with Scikit-Learn

```
from sklearn.svm import OneClassSVM
import numpy as np
import pandas as pd

# Sample data
data = pd.DataFrame({
    'Feature1': [1, 2, 3, 4, 5, 100],
    'Feature2': [1, 2, 3, 4, 5, 200]
})

# Initialize One-Class SVM
oc_svm    =    OneClassSVM(nu=0.1,    kernel='rbf',
gamma=0.1)

# Fit the model
oc_svm.fit(data)
```

```
# Predict anomalies
anomalies = oc_svm.predict(data)

# Convert predictions to a DataFrame
data['Anomaly'] = anomalies
data['Anomaly'] = data['Anomaly'].map({1: 'Normal', -
1: 'Anomaly'})

print("One-Class SVM Anomaly Detection:")
print(data)
```

Choosing the Right Anomaly Detection Technique

- **Isolation Forest**: Effective for large datasets and works well with high-dimensional data. It is less sensitive to parameter tuning and provides an efficient method for detecting anomalies.
- **One-Class SVM**: Suitable for high-dimensional data and performs well when the data is not uniformly distributed. It may require careful parameter tuning, particularly for the kernel and gamma values.

Applications of Anomaly Detection

1. **Fraud Detection**: Identifying fraudulent transactions or activities in financial systems.
2. **Network Security**: Detecting unusual network traffic that may indicate a security breach.

3. **Fault Detection**: Monitoring industrial systems to identify equipment failures or malfunctions.

4. **Health Monitoring**: Detecting anomalies in medical data to identify potential health issues.

Anomaly detection is a powerful tool for identifying unusual patterns in data that may indicate critical issues. Techniques like Isolation Forests and One-Class SVM offer effective methods for detecting anomalies, each with its strengths and specific applications. By leveraging Scikit-Learn's implementation of these techniques, you can build robust models for various anomaly detection tasks, enhancing your ability to address real-world problems and improve system performance.

Chapter 18

Natural Language Processing with Scikit-Learn

Natural Language Processing (NLP) is a field of artificial intelligence focused on the interaction between computers and human language. It encompasses various tasks, from text classification to sentiment analysis. This chapter explores key techniques for processing and analyzing text data, including feature extraction methods like TF-IDF and bag-of-words, and demonstrates how to build text classification models using Scikit-Learn's pipelines.

Introduction to Text Data Processing

Text data processing involves converting raw text into a format suitable for machine learning algorithms. This typically includes several steps: tokenization, normalization, and feature extraction.

Key Steps in Text Data Processing:

- **Tokenization**: Splitting text into individual words or tokens.
- **Normalization**: Converting text to a consistent format, such as lowercasing and removing punctuation.
- **Feature Extraction**: Converting text into numerical representations that can be used by machine learning models.

Feature Extraction Techniques

Feature extraction is a critical step in NLP, transforming text data into numerical features. Two common methods are the bag-of-words model and Term Frequency-Inverse Document Frequency (TF-IDF).

Bag-of-Words Model

The bag-of-words model represents text data as a collection of words and their frequencies, disregarding the order of words. This approach creates a document-term matrix, where rows represent documents and columns represent terms.

How Bag-of-Words Works:

1. **Tokenization**: Split text into individual words or tokens.
2. **Vocabulary Creation**: Build a vocabulary of unique words from the entire dataset.
3. **Vectorization**: Convert each document into a vector based on the frequency of words in the vocabulary.

Implementation with Scikit-Learn

```
from        sklearn.feature_extraction.text        import
CountVectorizer

# Sample documents
documents = [
    "Natural language processing is fun.",
```

```
    "I enjoy learning about machine learning.",
    "Text classification is a common NLP task."
]

# Initialize CountVectorizer
vectorizer = CountVectorizer()

# Fit and transform the documents
X = vectorizer.fit_transform(documents)

# Convert to DataFrame for better readability
import pandas as pd
df            =            pd.DataFrame(X.toarray(),
columns=vectorizer.get_feature_names_out())

print("Bag-of-Words Model:")
print(df)
```

TF-IDF (Term Frequency-Inverse Document Frequency)

TF-IDF improves upon the bag-of-words model by considering both the frequency of terms in a document (Term Frequency) and the inverse frequency of terms across all documents (Inverse Document Frequency). This helps in highlighting important terms and reducing the impact of commonly occurring words.

How TF-IDF Works:

1. **Term Frequency (TF)**: Measures how frequently a term occurs in a document.
2. **Inverse Document Frequency (IDF)**: Measures how important a term is by considering how frequently it appears across all documents.
3. **TF-IDF Score**: Combines TF and IDF to give a score that reflects the importance of a term in a document.

Implementation with Scikit-Learn

```
from        sklearn.feature_extraction.text        import
TfidfVectorizer

# Initialize TfidfVectorizer
tfidf_vectorizer = TfidfVectorizer()

# Fit and transform the documents
X_tfidf = tfidf_vectorizer.fit_transform(documents)

# Convert to DataFrame for better readability
df_tfidf       =        pd.DataFrame(X_tfidf.toarray(),
columns=tfidf_vectorizer.get_feature_names_out())

print("TF-IDF Model:")
print(df_tfidf)
```

Building Text Classification Models

Text classification involves assigning categories to text data based on its content. Common algorithms for text classification include Logistic Regression, Naive

170

Bayes, and Support Vector Machines (SVM). Scikit-Learn's pipelines streamline the process of building and evaluating these models.

Creating a Pipeline for Text Classification

A pipeline in Scikit-Learn allows you to streamline the process of text data processing, feature extraction, and model training. It combines multiple steps into a single workflow.

Steps in Building a Text Classification Pipeline:

1. **Text Processing**: Use CountVectorizer or TfidfVectorizer to convert text data into numerical features.
2. **Model Training**: Apply a classification algorithm to train a model on the extracted features.
3. **Evaluation**: Assess the performance of the model using evaluation metrics.

Implementation with Scikit-Learn

```
from sklearn.pipeline import Pipeline
from sklearn.naive_bayes import MultinomialNB
from sklearn.model_selection import train_test_split
from sklearn import metrics

# Sample documents and labels
documents = [
    "Natural language processing is fun.",
    "I enjoy learning about machine learning.",
```

```python
    "Text classification is a common NLP task.",
    "This movie is fantastic.",
    "I did not like this film."
]
labels = ['NLP', 'ML', 'NLP', 'Positive', 'Negative']

# Split data into training and testing sets
X_train, X_test, y_train, y_test = train_test_split(documents, labels, test_size=0.2, random_state=0)

# Initialize pipeline
pipeline = Pipeline([
    ('vectorizer', TfidfVectorizer()), # Feature extraction
    ('classifier', MultinomialNB())    # Classification model
])

# Train the model
pipeline.fit(X_train, y_train)

# Predict on the test date
y_pred = pipeline.predict(X_test)

# Evaluate the model
accuracy = metrics.accuracy_score(y_test, y_pred)

print("Text Classification Results:")
print("Predictions:", y_pred)
```

```
print("Accuracy:", accuracy)
```

Advanced Text Processing Techniques

In addition to the basic techniques discussed, several advanced methods can enhance text processing and classification:

- **N-grams**: Capture sequences of n words to understand context better.
- **Word Embeddings**: Represent words as vectors in a continuous space, capturing semantic relationships.
- **Named Entity Recognition (NER)**: Identify and classify entities such as names, dates, and locations in text.

Implementation with Scikit-Learn

For n-grams, you can modify the CountVectorizer or TfidfVectorizer to include them:

```python
# Initialize TfidfVectorizer with n-grams
ngram_vectorizer = TfidfVectorizer(ngram_range=(1, 2)) # Unigrams and bigrams

# Fit and transform the documents
X_ngram = ngram_vectorizer.fit_transform(documents)

# Convert to DataFrame for better readability
```

173

```
df_ngram       =       pd.DataFrame(X_ngram.toarray(),
columns=ngram_vectorizer.get_feature_names_out())

print("TF-IDF Model with N-grams:")
print(df_ngram)
```

Natural Language Processing (NLP) is a powerful tool for extracting meaningful information from text data. By mastering feature extraction techniques like TF-IDF and bag-of-words and utilizing Scikit-Learn's pipelines for building text classification models, you can develop robust NLP applications. These methods not only simplify the process but also enhance the performance of models in understanding and processing human language.

Chapter 19

Introduction to Neural Networks with Scikit-Learn

Neural networks, a fundamental component of deep learning, have transformed how complex patterns are recognized in data. This chapter provides an introduction to neural networks, focusing on their conceptual foundations, implementation of basic feedforward neural networks using Scikit-Learn, and the contexts in which neural networks offer advantages over traditional models.

Conceptual Understanding of Neural Networks

Neural networks are computational models inspired by the human brain's neural structure. They consist of interconnected nodes (neurons) organized into layers: input, hidden, and output layers. Each connection between neurons has a weight that adjusts as the network learns from data.

Key Concepts:

- **Neurons**: Basic units of a neural network, each applying a transformation to input data and passing it to the next layer.
- **Layers**: Composed of multiple neurons. Neural networks generally have three types of layers:
  - **Input Layer**: Receives input data.

- ○ **Hidden Layers**: Intermediate layers that process inputs through weights and activation functions.
- ○ **Output Layer**: Produces the final output, which can be a classification or regression result.
- **Activation Functions**: Functions applied to the output of neurons to introduce non-linearity, enabling the network to learn complex patterns. Common activation functions include ReLU (Rectified Linear Unit), Sigmoid, and Tanh.
- **Weights and Biases**: Parameters adjusted during training to minimize the error between predicted and actual outcomes.
- **Forward Propagation**: The process of passing input data through the network to obtain predictions.
- **Backpropagation**: The process of updating weights based on the error between predicted and actual outcomes, using gradient descent.

Implementing Basic Feedforward Neural Networks with Scikit-Learn

Scikit-Learn provides a simple interface for creating and training neural networks using the MLPClassifier and MLPRegressor classes. These classes implement a feedforward neural network with backpropagation for training.

Feedforward Neural Network Structure

A feedforward neural network consists of layers where each layer is connected to the next, and information flows in one direction—from input to output. The network learns by adjusting weights to reduce the error in predictions.

Key Components:

- **Hidden Layers**: Layers between the input and output layers, which help capture complex patterns.
- **Activation Function**: Typically, ReLU is used in hidden layers, while Sigmoid or Softmax is used in the output layer for classification tasks.

Implementation with Scikit-Learn

Below is an example of implementing a basic feedforward neural network using Scikit-Learn's MLPClassifier. This example demonstrates how to train the network for a classification task.

```
from sklearn.neural_network import MLPClassifier
from sklearn.datasets import load_iris
from sklearn.model_selection import train_test_split
from sklearn import metrics

# Load sample dataset
data = load_iris()
X, y = data.data, data.target

# Split data into training and testing sets
```

```
X_train, X_test, y_train, y_test = train_test_split(X, y,
test_size=0.2, random_state=42)

# Initialize the neural network model
mlp  =  MLPClassifier(hidden_layer_sizes=(10,  5),
activation='relu',   solver='adam',   max_iter=1000,
random_state=42)

# Train the model
mlp.fit(X_train, y_train)

# Predict on the test data
y_pred = mlp.predict(X_test)

# Evaluate the model
accuracy = metrics.accuracy_score(y_test, y_pred)

print("Neural Network Classification Results:")
print("Predictions:", y_pred)
print("Accuracy:", accuracy)
```

When to Use Neural Networks Over Traditional Models

Neural networks are particularly useful in scenarios where traditional models struggle to capture complex patterns or relationships in data. Here's a comparative view:

Advantages of Neural Networks:

- **Complex Pattern Recognition**: Capable of modeling intricate relationships and interactions within the data, especially in high-dimensional spaces.
- **Feature Learning**: Automatically learn useful features from raw data, reducing the need for manual feature engineering.
- **Scalability**: Effective with large datasets and can leverage large-scale computations on GPUs.

Limitations of Neural Networks:

- **Training Time**: Requires more computational resources and time compared to traditional models.
- **Overfitting**: Prone to overfitting, especially with small datasets or complex architectures.
- **Interpretability**: Models are often considered "black boxes," making it challenging to interpret how decisions are made.

Traditional Models vs. Neural Networks:

- **Linear Models**: Simple and interpretable, but limited to linear relationships. Ideal for smaller datasets or when interpretability is crucial.
- **Decision Trees and Random Forests**: Handle non-linearity and interactions well but may not perform as well on complex patterns as neural networks.

Advanced Topics in Neural Networks

As you advance, you may explore more complex neural network architectures and techniques:

- **Convolutional Neural Networks (CNNs)**: Specialized for image and spatial data processing.
- **Recurrent Neural Networks (RNNs)**: Suitable for sequential data, such as time series and natural language.
- **Deep Learning**: Involves using multiple layers (deep architectures) to capture hierarchical patterns.

Exploring Neural Networks Further

To deepen your understanding, consider experimenting with:

- **Hyperparameter Tuning**: Adjusting parameters such as the number of hidden layers, units per layer, and learning rates to optimize performance.
- **Regularization Techniques**: Techniques like dropout and L2 regularization to prevent overfitting.
- **Transfer Learning**: Leveraging pre-trained models and fine-tuning them for specific tasks.

Neural networks represent a powerful approach for learning and predicting complex patterns in data. By understanding their fundamental concepts and implementing basic feedforward neural networks with Scikit-Learn, you can leverage their capabilities for various tasks. As you advance, exploring more sophisticated architectures and techniques will further enhance your ability to tackle diverse machine learning problems.

Chapter 20

Deep Learning with Scikit-Learn and TensorFlow Integration

Deep learning has revolutionized the field of machine learning by enabling models to learn and represent complex patterns from large datasets. TensorFlow, an open-source deep learning framework, provides robust tools for building and training deep neural networks. Integrating TensorFlow with Scikit-Learn can leverage the strengths of both libraries, enabling a streamlined workflow for building and fine-tuning sophisticated models. This chapter explores how to combine Scikit-Learn with TensorFlow for deep learning applications, providing practical examples and strategies.

Introduction to Deep Learning

Deep learning involves using neural networks with multiple layers (deep neural networks) to model complex relationships in data. It excels in areas such as image recognition, natural language processing, and time series forecasting. Key concepts include:

- **Neural Networks**: Networks with multiple hidden layers between input and output.
- **Activation Functions**: Functions such as ReLU, Sigmoid, and Tanh introduce non-linearity.

- **Optimization**: Algorithms like gradient descent adjust weights to minimize the loss function.
- **Backpropagation**: A method for updating weights based on the error from predictions.

Overview of TensorFlow

TensorFlow is a popular deep learning framework developed by Google. It offers extensive functionalities for creating, training, and evaluating neural networks. Key components include:

- **Tensors**: Multi-dimensional arrays used for computation.
- **Keras API**: A high-level API within TensorFlow for building and training models.
- **Computational Graphs**: Graphs representing operations and data flow for efficient computation.

Integrating Scikit-Learn with TensorFlow

Integrating Scikit-Learn with TensorFlow allows you to harness the capabilities of both libraries. Scikit-Learn provides utilities for data preprocessing, model evaluation, and pipelines, while TensorFlow offers advanced deep learning capabilities. This integration can streamline workflows and enhance model development.

Creating a Pipeline with Scikit-Learn and TensorFlow

Scikit-Learn's Pipeline and GridSearchCV can be used to integrate TensorFlow models, enabling seamless preprocessing and hyperparameter tuning.

Example Workflow:

1. **Data Preprocessing**: Use Scikit-Learn for tasks such as scaling and splitting data.
2. **Model Building**: Create a deep learning model using TensorFlow.
3. **Integration**: Combine preprocessing and model in a Scikit-Learn pipeline.
4. **Hyperparameter Tuning**: Use Scikit-Learn's tools to tune model parameters.

Implementation Example

Here's how you can integrate a TensorFlow model into a Scikit-Learn pipeline for a classification task using the Keras API:

```
from sklearn.pipeline import Pipeline
from sklearn.preprocessing import StandardScaler
from sklearn.model_selection import train_test_split, GridSearchCV
from sklearn.metrics import accuracy_score
from tensorflow.keras.models import Sequential
from tensorflow.keras.layers import Dense
from tensorflow.keras.wrappers.scikit_learn import KerasClassifier
```

```python
# Define a function to create the Keras model
def create_model(activation='relu', optimizer='adam'):
    model = Sequential()
    model.add(Dense(12,                         input_dim=8,
activation=activation))
    model.add(Dense(8, activation=activation))
    model.add(Dense(1, activation='sigmoid'))
    model.compile(loss='binary_crossentropy',
optimizer=optimizer, metrics=['accuracy'])
    return model

# Create a KerasClassifier wrapper
model    =    KerasClassifier(build_fn=create_model,
verbose=0)

# Create the Scikit-Learn pipeline
pipeline = Pipeline([
    ('scaler', StandardScaler()),  # Preprocessing step
    ('model', model)               # TensorFlow model
])

# Load dataset
from sklearn.datasets import load_breast_cancer
data = load_breast_cancer()
X, y = data.data, data.target

# Split data
X_train, X_test, y_train, y_test = train_test_split(X, y,
test_size=0.2, random_state=42)
```

```python
# Define hyperparameters for GridSearchCV
param_grid = {
    'model__activation': ['relu', 'tanh'],
    'model__optimizer': ['adam', 'sgd']
}

# Initialize GridSearchCV
grid           =           GridSearchCV(estimator=pipeline,
param_grid=param_grid, cv=3, verbose=1, n_jobs=-1)

# Train the model
grid_result = grid.fit(X_train, y_train)

# Evaluate the model
y_pred = grid.predict(X_test)
accuracy = accuracy_score(y_test, y_pred)

print("Best Parameters:", grid_result.best_params_)
print("Accuracy:", accuracy)
```

Benefits of Integration

1. Unified Workflow: Combining Scikit-Learn and TensorFlow allows for a seamless workflow that integrates data preprocessing, model training, and evaluation. **2. Flexibility**: Use Scikit-Learn's tools for tasks like cross-validation and hyperparameter tuning with TensorFlow models. **3. Efficiency**: Leverage

Scikit-Learn's efficient data handling and TensorFlow's powerful deep learning capabilities.

Advanced Topics in Deep Learning with TensorFlow

For more complex applications, consider exploring:

- **Convolutional Neural Networks (CNNs)**: For image and spatial data processing.
- **Recurrent Neural Networks (RNNs)**: For sequential data, such as time series and text.
- **Transfer Learning**: Using pre-trained models and fine-tuning them for specific tasks.

Example: CNN with TensorFlow

Here's a brief example of using TensorFlow to build a Convolutional Neural Network (CNN) for image classification:

```python
from tensorflow.keras.datasets import mnist
from tensorflow.keras.utils import to_categorical

# Load dataset
(X_train, y_train), (X_test, y_test) = mnist.load_data()
X_train = X_train.reshape(X_train.shape[0], 28, 28, 1).astype('float32') / 255
X_test = X_test.reshape(X_test.shape[0], 28, 28, 1).astype('float32') / 255
y_train = to_categorical(y_train)
```

```python
y_test = to_categorical(y_test)

# Define CNN model
def create_cnn_model():
    model = Sequential()
    model.add(Dense(32,                    activation='relu',
input_shape=(28, 28, 1)))
    model.add(Dense(64, activation='relu'))
    model.add(Dense(10, activation='softmax'))
    model.compile(optimizer='adam',
loss='categorical_crossentropy', metrics=['accuracy'])
    return model

# Train and evaluate CNN model
cnn_model = create_cnn_model()
cnn_model.fit(X_train,        y_train,        epochs=10,
batch_size=64, validation_split=0.2)
score = cnn_model.evaluate(X_test, y_test)

print("CNN Test Loss:", score[0])
print("CNN Test Accuracy:", score[1])
```

Integrating Scikit-Learn with TensorFlow bridges the gap between traditional machine learning and advanced deep learning techniques. By combining Scikit-Learn's preprocessing and model evaluation capabilities with TensorFlow's powerful deep learning framework, you can build and fine-tune complex models more efficiently. This integration not only enhances your ability to tackle a wide range of machine learning problems but also streamlines the development process, making it easier to achieve high-impact results.

Building Custom Transformers and Pipelines

Scikit-Learn's pipeline feature is a powerful tool for creating a streamlined workflow for data preprocessing and model training. It allows you to encapsulate a sequence of data transformations and model fitting into a single, reusable object. This chapter focuses on mastering Scikit-Learn's pipeline functionality and building custom transformers to cater to specific preprocessing needs.

Understanding Scikit-Learn Pipelines

Pipelines in Scikit-Learn are used to streamline the process of applying a sequence of data transformations followed by model training. This approach promotes modularity and ensures that the same data preprocessing steps are applied consistently during both training and prediction. Key components include:

- **Steps**: Each step in a pipeline consists of a name and an object that performs a specific task (e.g., a transformer or estimator).
- **Transformers**: Objects that implement the fit and transform methods to modify data.

189

- **Estimators**: Objects that implement the fit and predict methods to build and use models.

Building a Basic Pipeline

To illustrate the concept, consider a simple pipeline that scales features and then fits a logistic regression model:

```
from sklearn.pipeline import Pipeline
from sklearn.preprocessing import StandardScaler
from sklearn.linear_model import LogisticRegression
from sklearn.datasets import load_iris
from sklearn.model_selection import train_test_split

# Load dataset
data = load_iris()
X, y = data.data, data.target

# Split data
X_train, X_test, y_train, y_test = train_test_split(X, y, test_size=0.2, random_state=42)

# Create a pipeline
pipeline = Pipeline([
    ('scaler', StandardScaler()),  # Feature scaling
    ('classifier', LogisticRegression())  # Model fitting
])

# Train the model
pipeline.fit(X_train, y_train)
```

```
# Make predictions
predictions = pipeline.predict(X_test)

# Print predictions
print("Predictions:", predictions)
```

This pipeline first scales the data using StandardScaler and then fits a LogisticRegression model. The advantage of using a pipeline is that it ensures consistent application of preprocessing steps.

Creating Custom Transformers

Custom transformers can be created to handle specific data preprocessing tasks that are not covered by Scikit-Learn's built-in transformers. To build a custom transformer, you need to define a class that implements the fit and transform methods.

Example: Custom Imputer

Suppose you need a custom imputer that fills missing values with the median of each feature. Here's how you can create and use such a transformer:

```
import numpy as np
from sklearn.base import BaseEstimator,
TransformerMixin
```

```python
class                    CustomImputer(BaseEstimator,
TransformerMixin):
    def __init__(self):
        self.medians_ = None

    def fit(self, X, y=None):
        self.medians_ = np.nanmedian(X, axis=0)
        return self

    def transform(self, X):
        X = np.array(X)
        X = np.where(np.isnan(X), self.medians_, X)
        return X

# Example usage
from sklearn.datasets import load_iris
from sklearn.pipeline import Pipeline
from sklearn.linear_model import LogisticRegression
from sklearn.model_selection import train_test_split

# Load dataset
data = load_iris()
X, y = data.data, data.target

# Introduce some NaNs
X[0, 0] = np.nan

# Create a pipeline with the custom imputer
pipeline = Pipeline([
```

```
    ('imputer', CustomImputer()),  # Custom imputer
    ('classifier', LogisticRegression())  # Model fitting
])

# Split data
X_train, X_test, y_train, y_test = train_test_split(X, y,
test_size=0.2, random_state=42)

# Train the model
pipeline.fit(X_train, y_train)

# Make predictions
predictions = pipeline.predict(X_test)

# Print predictions
print("Predictions:", predictions)
```

In this example, CustomImputer replaces missing values with the median of each feature. This custom transformer is integrated into the pipeline, ensuring that missing values are handled appropriately before model training.

Combining Custom Transformers in a Pipeline

You can build more complex pipelines by combining multiple custom transformers. For instance, consider a pipeline that performs feature scaling, custom imputation, and model fitting:

```python
from sklearn.preprocessing import StandardScaler
from sklearn.linear_model import LogisticRegression
from sklearn.datasets import load_iris
from sklearn.model_selection import train_test_split

# Define the custom imputer
class CustomImputer(BaseEstimator, TransformerMixin):
    def __init__(self):
        self.medians_ = None

    def fit(self, X, y=None):
        self.medians_ = np.nanmedian(X, axis=0)
        return self

    def transform(self, X):
        X = np.array(X)
        X = np.where(np.isnan(X), self.medians_, X)
        return X

# Load dataset
data = load_iris()
X, y = data.data, data.target

# Introduce some NaNs
X[0, 0] = np.nan

# Create a pipeline with multiple custom transformers
pipeline = Pipeline([
```

```python
    ('imputer', CustomImputer()),  # Custom imputer
    ('scaler', StandardScaler()),  # Feature scaling
    ('classifier', LogisticRegression())  # Model fitting
])

# Split data
X_train, X_test, y_train, y_test = train_test_split(X, y,
test_size=0.2, random_state=42)

# Train the model
pipeline.fit(X_train, y_train)

# Make predictions
predictions = pipeline.predict(X_test)

# Print predictions
print("Predictions:", predictions)
```

Benefits of Using Pipelines and Custom Transformers

1. Consistency: Pipelines ensure that the same preprocessing steps are applied during both training and prediction. **2. Modularity**: Custom transformers allow for the creation of reusable components tailored to specific needs. **3. Reproducibility**: Pipelines facilitate reproducible experiments by encapsulating the complete preprocessing and modeling process.

Advanced Custom Transformers

For more advanced use cases, consider creating transformers that:

- **Feature Extraction**: Extract specific features from raw data, such as text or images.
- **Dimensionality Reduction**: Implement custom dimensionality reduction techniques.
- **Feature Engineering**: Perform specialized feature engineering tasks, such as polynomial feature generation.

Example: Custom Feature Engineering Transformer

Here's an example of a custom transformer that creates polynomial features:

```python
from sklearn.base import BaseEstimator, TransformerMixin
from sklearn.preprocessing import PolynomialFeatures

class CustomPolynomialFeatures(BaseEstimator, TransformerMixin):
    def __init__(self, degree=2):
        self.degree = degree
        self.poly = PolynomialFeatures(degree)

    def fit(self, X, y=None):
        self.poly.fit(X)
        return self
```

```python
    def transform(self, X):
        return self.poly.transform(X)

# Example usage
from sklearn.datasets import load_iris
from sklearn.pipeline import Pipeline
from sklearn.linear_model import LogisticRegression
from sklearn.model_selection import train_test_split

# Load dataset
data = load_iris()
X, y = data.data, data.target

# Create a pipeline with custom polynomial features
pipeline = Pipeline([
    ('poly', CustomPolynomialFeatures(degree=3)),    #
Polynomial feature generation
    ('scaler', StandardScaler()),  # Feature scaling
    ('classifier', LogisticRegression())  # Model fitting
])

# Split data
X_train, X_test, y_train, y_test = train_test_split(X, y,
test_size=0.2, random_state=42)

# Train the model
pipeline.fit(X_train, y_train)

# Make predictions
```

```
predictions = pipeline.predict(X_test)

# Print predictions
print("Predictions:", predictions)
```

Building custom transformers and pipelines in Scikit-Learn enhances the flexibility and efficiency of your machine learning workflows. By encapsulating data transformations and model fitting into reusable components, you ensure consistency, modularity, and reproducibility. This chapter has provided practical examples of creating and integrating custom transformers into pipelines, paving the way for more advanced and tailored machine learning solutions.

Chapter 21

Time Series Forecasting with Machine Learning

Time series forecasting involves predicting future values based on previously observed values, and it is crucial in various fields such as finance, economics, and supply chain management. In this chapter, we explore how to apply Scikit-Learn to time series data for forecasting. We will discuss the core concepts of time series analysis and delve into implementing algorithms such as ARIMA, Prophet, and Random Forest Regressors.

Understanding Time Series Data

Time series data consists of observations recorded sequentially over time. Key characteristics of time series data include:

- **Trend**: Long-term movement in the data.
- **Seasonality**: Regular pattern or cycle in the data, often influenced by seasonal factors.
- **Noise**: Random variation in the data that cannot be attributed to trend or seasonality.

Time Series Analysis and Preprocessing

Before applying machine learning models, it's crucial to preprocess time series data:

1. Handling Missing Values

Time series data can have missing values due to various reasons. Techniques to handle missing values include:

- **Interpolation**: Estimating missing values based on available data points.
- **Forward/Backward Fill**: Using previous or next observations to fill missing values.

2. Differencing

Differencing helps in stabilizing the mean of a time series by subtracting the previous observation from the current observation. This process is useful in making the series stationary.

```python
import pandas as pd

# Sample time series data
data = pd.Series([1, 3, 2, 5, 7, 8, 12, 13, 15],
name='value')

# Difference the series
diff_data = data.diff().dropna()
print(diff_data)
```

ARIMA (AutoRegressive Integrated Moving Average)

ARIMA is a popular model for time series forecasting. It combines autoregression (AR), differencing (I), and moving averages (MA) to capture temporal dependencies in the data.

1. Implementing ARIMA

ARIMA requires the following steps:

- **Stationarity Check**: Use tests like the Dickey-Fuller test to check for stationarity.
- **Model Fitting**: Fit the ARIMA model to the data using statsmodels.

```python
from statsmodels.tsa.arima_model import ARIMA
import pandas as pd

# Sample time series data
data = pd.Series([1, 3, 2, 5, 7, 8, 12, 13, 15])

# Fit ARIMA model
model = ARIMA(data, order=(1, 1, 1))  # (p, d, q)
model_fit = model.fit(disp=0)

# Forecast
forecast = model_fit.forecast(steps=3)[0]
print("ARIMA Forecast:", forecast)
```

2. Model Diagnostics

Evaluate the ARIMA model using diagnostic plots and tests to ensure the model fits the data well and residuals are white noise.

```python
import matplotlib.pyplot as plt

# Plot diagnostics
model_fit.plot_diagnostics(figsize=(10, 8))
plt.show()
```

Prophet

Prophet is a forecasting tool developed by Facebook, designed to handle time series data with strong seasonal effects and missing data.

1. Implementing Prophet

Prophet requires the data to be in a specific format with columns ds for dates and y for values.

```python
from fbprophet import Prophet
import pandas as pd

# Prepare data
df = pd.DataFrame({
    'ds': pd.date_range(start='2023-01-01', periods=9, freq='D'),
    'y': [1, 3, 2, 5, 7, 8, 12, 13, 15]
})
```

```
# Initialize and fit Prophet model
model = Prophet()
model.fit(df)

# Forecast
future = model.make_future_dataframe(periods=3)
forecast = model.predict(future)
model.plot(forecast)
plt.show()
```

Random Forest Regressors

Random Forest Regressors are ensemble learning models that use multiple decision trees to improve forecasting accuracy. They can handle time series data by including lagged features.

1. Implementing Random Forest Regressors

To use Random Forest Regressors for time series forecasting:

- **Feature Engineering**: Create lagged features from the time series data.
- **Model Training**: Train the Random Forest Regressor using Scikit-Learn.

```
from sklearn.ensemble import RandomForestRegressor
from sklearn.model_selection import train_test_split
import pandas as pd
```

```python
# Create lagged features
data = pd.DataFrame({
    'value': [1, 3, 2, 5, 7, 8, 12, 13, 15]
})
data['lag1'] = data['value'].shift(1)
data = data.dropna()

# Split data
X = data[['lag1']]
y = data['value']
X_train, X_test, y_train, y_test = train_test_split(X, y,
test_size=0.2, random_state=42)

# Fit Random Forest Regressor
model = RandomForestRegressor()
model.fit(X_train, y_train)

# Forecast
forecast = model.predict(X_test)
print("Random Forest Forecast:", forecast)
```

Comparing Forecasting Models

When applying different forecasting models, it's essential to compare their performance using appropriate metrics:

- **Mean Absolute Error (MAE)**: Measures the average magnitude of errors in predictions.

- **Mean Squared Error (MSE)**: Measures the average squared difference between actual and predicted values.
- **Root Mean Squared Error (RMSE)**: Provides the square root of MSE, giving error in the same units as the target variable.

```python
from sklearn.metrics import mean_absolute_error,
mean_squared_error
import numpy as np

# Calculate metrics
mae = mean_absolute_error(y_test, forecast)
mse = mean_squared_error(y_test, forecast)
rmse = np.sqrt(mse)

print("MAE:", mae)
print("MSE:", mse)
print("RMSE:", rmse)
```

Time series forecasting with machine learning involves a range of techniques to predict future values based on past observations. By leveraging models such as ARIMA, Prophet, and Random Forest Regressors, and understanding the importance of preprocessing and feature engineering, you can effectively forecast time-dependent data. This chapter has provided an overview of applying these methods using Scikit-Learn and other relevant libraries, equipping you with the tools to handle various forecasting challenges.

Chapter 22

Using Scikit-Learn for Recommender Systems

Recommender systems are an essential component in modern applications, providing personalized recommendations to users based on their preferences and behaviors. Scikit-Learn offers various tools and techniques to build effective recommender systems, leveraging its machine learning capabilities. In this chapter, we will explore the fundamentals of recommender systems, focusing on collaborative filtering, content-based filtering, and hybrid approaches, and understand how to implement these techniques using Scikit-Learn.

Understanding Recommender Systems

Recommender systems are designed to suggest relevant items to users based on their preferences. They can be categorized into three primary types:

- **Collaborative Filtering**: Relies on user-item interactions and similarities between users or items.
- **Content-Based Filtering**: Uses item attributes and user preferences to make recommendations.
- **Hybrid Methods**: Combine collaborative and content-based approaches to improve recommendation quality.

Collaborative Filtering

Collaborative filtering is a popular approach that makes recommendations based on the behavior and preferences of similar users. There are two main types:

1. User-Based Collaborative Filtering

User-based collaborative filtering recommends items to a user based on the preferences of similar users. The core idea is to find users with similar tastes and suggest items they liked.

Implementation Using Scikit-Learn

Scikit-Learn does not directly provide user-based collaborative filtering, but we can use similarity measures and clustering techniques to build such a system.

```python
import numpy as np
from sklearn.metrics.pairwise import cosine_similarity
from sklearn.preprocessing import StandardScaler

# Sample user-item rating matrix
ratings = np.array([[5, 3, 0, 1],
            [4, 0, 0, 1],
            [1, 1, 0, 5],
            [0, 0, 5, 4],
            [2, 4, 3, 0]])

# Standardize the ratings
scaler = StandardScaler()
```

```
ratings_scaled = scaler.fit_transform(ratings)

# Compute similarity between users
user_similarity = cosine_similarity(ratings_scaled)

print("User Similarity Matrix:\n", user_similarity)
```

2. Item-Based Collaborative Filtering

Item-based collaborative filtering recommends items based on similarities between items rather than users. This approach often involves calculating item-item similarity and recommending items similar to those the user has liked.

Implementation Using Scikit-Learn

```
from sklearn.metrics.pairwise import cosine_similarity

# Compute similarity between items
item_similarity = cosine_similarity(ratings.T)

print("Item Similarity Matrix:\n", item_similarity)
```

Content-Based Filtering

Content-based filtering recommends items based on the features of items and the preferences of the user. It relies on analyzing the attributes of items and comparing them to user profiles.

1. Feature Extraction

To implement content-based filtering, you need to extract features from items. For example, if recommending movies, features could include genres, actors, and directors.

Implementation Using Scikit-Learn

```
from        sklearn.feature_extraction.text        import
TfidfVectorizer

# Sample item descriptions
descriptions   =   ["Action   adventure   movie   with
superheroes",
          "Romantic comedy with a love story",
          "Sci-fi thriller with space travel",
          "Documentary about nature and wildlife"]

# Convert descriptions to TF-IDF features
vectorizer = TfidfVectorizer()
tfidf_matrix = vectorizer.fit_transform(descriptions)

print("TF-IDF Matrix:\n", tfidf_matrix.toarray())
```

2. User Profile Building

Build a user profile based on their interactions or preferences, and compare it with item features to make recommendations.

Implementation Using Scikit-Learn

```python
from sklearn.metrics.pairwise import cosine_similarity

# Sample user profile (e.g., preferences for action and sci-fi)
user_profile = vectorizer.transform(["Action adventure movie", "Sci-fi thriller"])

# Compute similarity between user profile and items
profile_similarity = cosine_similarity(user_profile, tfidf_matrix)

print("Profile Similarity:\n", profile_similarity)
```

Hybrid Recommendation Approaches

Hybrid recommender systems combine collaborative filtering and content-based filtering to leverage the strengths of both methods and mitigate their individual weaknesses.

1. Combining Approaches

A common hybrid approach is to blend the recommendations from collaborative filtering and content-based filtering. This can be achieved by combining similarity scores or using ensemble methods.

Implementation Example

```
# Example weights for combining collaborative and
content-based scores
weight_cf = 0.5
weight_cb = 0.5

# Example similarity scores
user_sim = user_similarity[0]
item_sim = item_similarity[:, 0]
content_sim = profile_similarity.flatten()

# Combine scores
combined_scores = weight_cf * user_sim + weight_cb
* (content_sim + item_sim)

print("Combined        Recommendation        Scores:\n",
combined_scores)
```

Evaluating Recommender Systems

Evaluating the effectiveness of recommender systems
involves several metrics:

- **Precision and Recall**: Measure how many of the
  recommended items are relevant and how many
  relevant items are recommended.
- **F1 Score**: The harmonic mean of precision and recall.
- **Mean Absolute Error (MAE)**: Measures the average
  magnitude of errors in recommendations.

Implementation Using Scikit-Learn

```python
from sklearn.metrics import precision_recall_curve,
f1_score, mean_absolute_error

# Sample true and predicted relevance scores
true_relevance = np.array([1, 0, 1, 1, 0])
predicted_relevance = np.array([0.8, 0.2, 0.6, 0.9, 0.1])

# Precision, Recall, and F1 Score
precision,          recall,          _          =
precision_recall_curve(true_relevance,
predicted_relevance)
f1          =          f1_score(true_relevance,
predicted_relevance.round())

# Mean Absolute Error
mae     =     mean_absolute_error(true_relevance,
predicted_relevance)

print("Precision:", precision)
print("Recall:", recall)
print("F1 Score:", f1)
print("Mean Absolute Error:", mae)
```

Building effective recommender systems using Scikit-Learn involves understanding the core principles of collaborative filtering, content-based filtering, and hybrid approaches. By implementing these techniques and evaluating their performance, you can develop robust systems that provide valuable recommendations to users. This chapter has provided practical insights and examples to help you apply Scikit-Learn for creating and optimizing recommender systems.

Chapter 23

Model Performance Metrics and Interpretability

Evaluating machine learning models accurately is crucial to understanding their effectiveness and ensuring they meet the desired performance criteria. In this chapter, we will delve into essential metrics for assessing both classification and regression models. We will also explore techniques for model interpretability, such as SHAP and LIME, which help in understanding the predictions made by complex models.

Performance Metrics for Classification Models

Classification models predict categorical outcomes. Evaluating their performance involves several key metrics:

1. Confusion Matrix

A confusion matrix provides a comprehensive view of a model's performance by showing the true positives, true negatives, false positives, and false negatives. This matrix helps visualize how well a model distinguishes between different classes.

Implementation Using Scikit-Learn

```
from sklearn.metrics import confusion_matrix
import numpy as np
```

```python
# Sample true and predicted labels
y_true = np.array([0, 1, 0, 1, 0, 1, 1, 0])
y_pred = np.array([0, 1, 1, 1, 0, 0, 1, 1])

# Compute confusion matrix
cm = confusion_matrix(y_true, y_pred)

print("Confusion Matrix:\n", cm)
```

2. ROC Curve and AUC

The Receiver Operating Characteristic (ROC) curve plots the true positive rate against the false positive rate at various threshold settings. The Area Under the Curve (AUC) represents the model's ability to discriminate between positive and negative classes.

Implementation Using Scikit-Learn

```python
from sklearn.metrics import roc_curve, auc
import matplotlib.pyplot as plt

# Sample probabilities and true labels
y_prob = np.array([0.1, 0.4, 0.35, 0.8, 0.7, 0.6, 0.9, 0.2])
y_true = np.array([0, 1, 0, 1, 1, 0, 1, 0])

# Compute ROC curve
fpr, tpr, _ = roc_curve(y_true, y_prob)
roc_auc = auc(fpr, tpr)
```

```python
# Plot ROC curve
plt.figure()
plt.plot(fpr, tpr, color='darkorange', lw=2, label='ROC curve (area = %0.2f)' % roc_auc)
plt.plot([0, 1], [0, 1], color='navy', lw=2, linestyle='--')
plt.xlim([0.0, 1.0])
plt.ylim([0.0, 1.05])
plt.xlabel('False Positive Rate')
plt.ylabel('True Positive Rate')
plt.title('Receiver Operating Characteristic')
plt.legend(loc="lower right")
plt.show()

print("AUC:", roc_auc)
```

3. Precision-Recall Curve

The Precision-Recall curve illustrates the trade-off between precision (positive predictive value) and recall (sensitivity) for different thresholds. It is especially useful when dealing with imbalanced datasets.

Implementation Using Scikit-Learn

```python
from sklearn.metrics import precision_recall_curve
import matplotlib.pyplot as plt

# Sample probabilities and true labels
y_prob = np.array([0.1, 0.4, 0.35, 0.8, 0.7, 0.6, 0.9, 0.2])
```

```
y_true = np.array([0, 1, 0, 1, 1, 0, 1, 0])

# Compute Precision-Recall curve
precision, recall, _ = precision_recall_curve(y_true, y_prob)

# Plot Precision-Recall curve
plt.figure()
plt.plot(recall, precision, color='blue', lw=2)
plt.xlabel('Recall')
plt.ylabel('Precision')
plt.title('Precision-Recall Curve')
plt.show()
```

Performance Metrics for Regression Models

Regression models predict continuous outcomes, and their performance is evaluated using different metrics:

1. Mean Absolute Error (MAE)

The Mean Absolute Error measures the average magnitude of errors in predictions, providing an understanding of how close predictions are to the actual values.

Implementation Using Scikit-Learn

```
from sklearn.metrics import mean_absolute_error

# Sample true and predicted values
```

```
y_true = np.array([3.5, 2.1, 4.8, 3.9])
y_pred = np.array([3.6, 2.0, 4.7, 4.0])

# Compute Mean Absolute Error
mae = mean_absolute_error(y_true, y_pred)

print("Mean Absolute Error:", mae)
```

2. Mean Squared Error (MSE) and R^2 Score

The Mean Squared Error measures the average squared difference between predicted and actual values. The R^2 score indicates how well the model explains the variance in the target variable.

Implementation Using Scikit-Learn

```
from sklearn.metrics import mean_squared_error, r2_score

# Compute Mean Squared Error and R² score
mse = mean_squared_error(y_true, y_pred)
r2 = r2_score(y_true, y_pred)

print("Mean Squared Error:", mse)
print("R² Score:", r2)
```

Model Interpretability Techniques

219

Model interpretability is crucial for understanding how a model makes predictions and for ensuring transparency and trustworthiness.

1. SHAP (SHapley Additive exPlanations)

SHAP values provide insights into the contribution of each feature to the model's predictions. They are derived from cooperative game theory and help explain model behavior.

Implementation Using SHAP

```
import shap
from sklearn.ensemble import RandomForestClassifier

# Train a RandomForest model
model = RandomForestClassifier()
model.fit(X_train, y_train)

# Create a SHAP explainer
explainer = shap.TreeExplainer(model)
shap_values = explainer.shap_values(X_test)

# Plot SHAP values
shap.summary_plot(shap_values, X_test)
```

2. LIME (Local Interpretable Model-agnostic Explanations)

LIME provides local explanations for individual predictions by approximating the model with a simpler, interpretable model in the vicinity of a prediction.

Implementation Using LIME

```
import lime
import lime.lime_tabular

# Train a model
model = RandomForestClassifier()
model.fit(X_train, y_train)

# Create a LIME explainer
explainer                                    =
lime.lime_tabular.LimeTabularExplainer(X_train,
feature_names=feature_names, class_names=['class_0',
'class_1'])
i = 0  # Index of the instance to explain
explanation  =  explainer.explain_instance(X_test[i],
model.predict_proba)

# Plot LIME explanation
explanation.show_in_notebook()
```

Model performance metrics and interpretability techniques are critical for evaluating and understanding machine learning models. By leveraging confusion matrices, ROC curves, precision-recall curves, and metrics for regression models, you can gain a comprehensive view of your model's performance. Additionally, techniques like SHAP and LIME provide valuable insights into how models make predictions, ensuring transparency and trust in machine learning systems. This chapter has covered essential tools and techniques to assess and interpret models, laying the groundwork for effective machine learning practice.

Chapter 24

Model Deployment with Scikit-Learn: From Prototyping to Production

Deploying machine learning models into production involves transitioning from experimental prototypes to fully operational systems. This chapter explores the process of deploying models using Scikit-Learn, including techniques for model serialization, versioning, and exposing models via REST APIs. Understanding these aspects is crucial for integrating machine learning models into real-world applications and ensuring they deliver value in a production environment.

Model Serialization and Deserialization

Serialization is the process of saving a model to a file so it can be loaded and used later. Deserialization is the reverse process, where the saved model is loaded back into memory. Scikit-Learn supports serialization using Python's built-in pickle module and joblib, which is optimized for handling large numpy arrays.

1. Using joblib for Serialization

The joblib library is commonly used with Scikit-Learn for its efficiency in saving large models and numpy arrays. Here's how to serialize and deserialize a model using joblib:

Serialization Example:

```
import joblib
from sklearn.ensemble import RandomForestClassifier

# Train a model
model = RandomForestClassifier()
model.fit(X_train, y_train)

# Save the model to a file
joblib.dump(model, 'random_forest_model.pkl')
```

Deserialization Example:

```
import joblib

# Load the model from the file
loaded_model =
joblib.load('random_forest_model.pkl')

# Use the model for prediction
predictions = loaded_model.predict(X_test)
```

2. Using pickle for Serialization

While joblib is preferred for large models, the pickle module is another option for model serialization.

Serialization Example:

```python
import pickle
from sklearn.ensemble import RandomForestClassifier

# Train a model
model = RandomForestClassifier()
model.fit(X_train, y_train)

# Save the model to a file
with open('random_forest_model.pkl', 'wb') as file:
    pickle.dump(model, file)
```

Deserialization Example:

```python
import pickle

# Load the model from the file
with open('random_forest_model.pkl', 'rb') as file:
    loaded_model = pickle.load(file)

# Use the model for prediction
predictions = loaded_model.predict(X_test)
```

Model Versioning

Versioning is essential for managing changes to models over time and ensuring that you can track and reproduce results. Each model version should be tagged with a unique identifier to differentiate it from others.

1. Implementing Model Versioning

One approach to model versioning is to include version information in the filename or metadata. For example:

```
import joblib

version = "v1.0"
filename = f'random_forest_model_{version}.pkl'

# Save the model with version information
joblib.dump(model, filename)
```

2. Tracking Model Versions

Consider using a model management system or database to track different versions, including details such as training data, hyperparameters, and performance metrics.

Exposing Models via REST APIs

Exposing a machine learning model via a REST API allows applications to interact with the model over the web. This is often done using frameworks like Flask or FastAPI in Python.

1. Building a REST API with Flask

Flask is a lightweight web framework for Python that can be used to create REST APIs.

Example Flask API:

```python
from flask import Flask, request, jsonify
import joblib

app = Flask(__name__)

# Load the model
model = joblib.load('random_forest_model.pkl')

@app.route('/predict', methods=['POST'])
def predict():
    # Get JSON data from the request
    data = request.get_json()
    features = data['features']

    # Make a prediction
    prediction = model.predict([features])

    # Return the result as JSON
    return jsonify({'prediction': prediction[0]})

if __name__ == '__main__':
    app.run(debug=True)
```

Running the Flask API:

1. Save the code in a file, for example, app.py.
2. Run the Flask application with python app.py.
3. Access the API at http://127.0.0.1:5000/predict.

2. Building a REST API with FastAPI

FastAPI is a modern framework for building APIs with Python that offers faster performance and automatic documentation.

Example FastAPI API:

```python
from fastapi import FastAPI
from pydantic import BaseModel
import joblib

app = FastAPI()

# Load the model
model = joblib.load('random_forest_model.pkl')

class Features(BaseModel):
    features: list

@app.post('/predict')
def predict(features: Features):
    # Make a prediction
    prediction = model.predict([features.features])

    # Return the result as JSON
    return {'prediction': prediction[0]}

# To run the FastAPI server, use the command: uvicorn app:app --reload
```

Running the FastAPI API:

1. Save the code in a file, for example, app.py.
2. Run the FastAPI server with uvicorn app:app --reload.
3. Access the API at http://127.0.0.1:8000/predict.

Testing and Monitoring

Once deployed, it's crucial to test and monitor the model's performance in production:

1. Testing

Test the API endpoints using tools like Postman or cURL to ensure they handle requests and return correct responses.

2. Monitoring

Implement monitoring tools to track the performance and health of your model. This includes checking prediction accuracy, response times, and system resource usage.

Deploying machine learning models involves more than just training; it requires effective serialization, versioning, and exposing models via APIs. By using tools like joblib and pickle for serialization, incorporating versioning practices, and implementing REST APIs with Flask or FastAPI, you can transition from prototyping to production seamlessly. Additionally, testing and monitoring are vital for ensuring that deployed models continue to perform well and meet user needs. This chapter has provided a comprehensive guide to deploying Scikit-Learn models, setting the stage for integrating machine learning into real-world applications.

Managing Large Datasets: Scaling Scikit-Learn with Dask and Joblib

As machine learning practitioners work with increasingly large datasets, traditional computing approaches can struggle to handle the data's size and complexity. When datasets no longer fit into memory, and operations become slow, it's essential to look for ways to scale. This chapter covers techniques to scale Scikit-Learn workflows using Dask for distributed computing and Joblib for parallel processing. Both tools enhance performance when working with large datasets, enabling faster model training, tuning, and evaluation.

Challenges of Working with Large Datasets

Working with large datasets presents several challenges. First, the dataset might not fit into memory all at once, making it difficult to perform basic operations like loading and transforming data. Additionally, algorithms that work efficiently on small datasets may slow down significantly or fail altogether when applied to large datasets. These challenges necessitate strategies that allow computation across multiple processors or distributed systems.

1. Memory Limitations

Most personal computers have a limited amount of RAM. When the size of a dataset exceeds available memory, even loading the dataset into Python's environment can become impossible. In such cases, reading data in chunks, distributing the computation, or moving to a more powerful computational environment becomes necessary.

2. Computational Complexity

Machine learning algorithms have different time complexities. As dataset size increases, the time taken for training and prediction can grow significantly. Linear models, for example, scale linearly with the number of samples, but tree-based models or nearest neighbors may exhibit worse performance as dataset size grows. Scaling these operations by using parallel processing or distributed computing can alleviate the performance bottleneck.

Scaling Scikit-Learn with Joblib

Joblib is a Python library that extends Scikit-Learn's capability to perform parallel processing efficiently. Many Scikit-Learn models, such as ensemble methods and cross-validation, support parallel processing natively through Joblib. By distributing the computation across multiple CPU cores, Joblib can reduce the time it takes to train and evaluate models.

1. Enabling Parallel Processing with Joblib

In Scikit-Learn, Joblib is used internally for parallel tasks. For example, if you're working with a Random Forest classifier, you can enable parallel processing by setting the n_jobs parameter:

```
from sklearn.ensemble import RandomForestClassifier

# Create a RandomForestClassifier with parallel processing
rf_model = RandomForestClassifier(n_estimators=100, n_jobs=-1)

# Fit the model on training data
rf_model.fit(X_train, y_train)
```

In this case, setting n_jobs=-1 tells Scikit-Learn to use all available CPU cores for training the model. This results in significant performance improvements, especially when working with large datasets or performing time-consuming operations like grid search.

2. Joblib for Cross-Validation

Cross-validation is a technique for evaluating model performance by splitting the dataset into multiple training and testing subsets. When working with large datasets, cross-validation can become computationally expensive. By enabling parallel processing with Joblib, cross-validation can be significantly accelerated:

```python
from sklearn.model_selection import cross_val_score
from sklearn.ensemble import RandomForestClassifier

# Initialize the model
rf_model = RandomForestClassifier(n_estimators=100, n_jobs=-1)

# Perform cross-validation using all CPU cores
cv_scores = cross_val_score(rf_model, X, y, cv=5, n_jobs=-1)

print("Cross-validation scores:", cv_scores)
```

Here, the n_jobs=-1 parameter is passed to both the model and the cross-validation function, ensuring parallelism across all computations. This results in faster execution times, even when evaluating multiple folds of data.

Scaling Scikit-Learn with Dask

While Joblib can speed up computations on a single machine by leveraging all available CPU cores, Dask is designed for distributed computing and can handle much larger datasets. Dask enables users to scale beyond a single machine, distributing data and computation across multiple workers, either on local systems or in cloud environments.

1. What is Dask?

Dask is a flexible library for parallel computing in Python. It is designed to work with datasets that are too large to fit into memory. Dask provides a DataFrame API that mimics Pandas, but it operates on data that is stored across multiple machines or partitions, allowing you to load, process, and analyze datasets that wouldn't otherwise fit into memory.

2. Using Dask with Scikit-Learn

To use Dask with Scikit-Learn, you can leverage dask-ml, an extension of Scikit-Learn that supports parallel and distributed computation. By replacing the standard Scikit-Learn estimators with their Dask counterparts, you can scale your machine learning tasks to handle larger datasets.

For example, training a large dataset with Dask can be done using the ParallelPostFit module, which enables Scikit-Learn models to work seamlessly with Dask arrays or Dask DataFrames.

Example: Training with Dask:

```
import dask.dataframe as dd
from dask_ml.model_selection import train_test_split
```

```python
from dask_ml.wrappers import ParallelPostFit
from sklearn.ensemble import RandomForestClassifier

# Load a large dataset into a Dask DataFrame
df = dd.read_csv('large_dataset.csv')

# Split the dataset into training and testing sets
X_train, X_test, y_train, y_test =
train_test_split(df.iloc[:, :-1], df.iloc[:, -1])

# Initialize a Scikit-Learn model wrapped in
ParallelPostFit
rf_model =
ParallelPostFit(estimator=RandomForestClassifier(n_e
stimators=100))

# Train the model
rf_model.fit(X_train, y_train)

# Make predictions
predictions = rf_model.predict(X_test)
```

In this example, the dataset is loaded as a Dask DataFrame, allowing you to work with datasets that are larger than memory. The ParallelPostFit wrapper ensures that the Random Forest model can train on Dask arrays, while parallelizing the computation across available workers.

3. Dask's Lazy Evaluation

Dask uses lazy evaluation, meaning that it doesn't perform computations until they are explicitly triggered. This approach allows Dask to build computation graphs that can be optimized and executed in parallel, improving the efficiency of operations. For instance, when you call a method like .fit() on a Dask model, the operation is not immediately executed but queued until you request the result.

Best Practices for Handling Large Datasets

Managing large datasets efficiently involves more than just using tools like Dask and Joblib. Here are some best practices to ensure optimal performance:

1. Chunking Data

For datasets that don't fit into memory, loading and processing data in chunks can prevent memory overload. Libraries like Pandas allow you to read large CSV files in chunks:

```
for chunk in pd.read_csv('large_file.csv', chunksize=10000):
    process(chunk)
```

By processing data in smaller chunks, you can avoid loading the entire dataset into memory at once.

2. Feature Engineering Before Scaling

Before applying parallel or distributed processing, ensure that feature engineering steps (such as scaling, normalization, or one-hot encoding) are applied consistently. These steps can significantly impact model performance, and inconsistencies in the preprocessing pipeline may lead to inaccurate results.

3. Monitor Resource Usage

When working with large datasets, it's essential to monitor CPU, memory, and disk usage to avoid performance bottlenecks. Tools like dask.distributed provide a dashboard for monitoring distributed computations, allowing you to see the workload distribution and optimize it accordingly.

Scaling machine learning workflows to handle large datasets is critical in today's data-intensive world. By leveraging Joblib for parallel processing and Dask for distributed computing, Scikit-Learn users can extend the capabilities of their models to work efficiently with massive datasets. Whether working on a local machine or a distributed cluster, these tools offer flexibility and scalability, ensuring that machine learning pipelines remain performant even as data size grows.

Chapter 25

Ethics in Machine Learning: Bias Detection, Fairness, and Transparency

As machine learning becomes more integrated into our daily lives, the ethical considerations surrounding its development and use have gained significant attention. While these algorithms hold the promise of increasing efficiency and innovation, they also pose risks, including the potential for biased decision-making, lack of transparency, and unfair outcomes. In this chapter, we will discuss the ethical implications of machine learning, focusing on bias detection, fairness, and transparency. We will also explore how Scikit-Learn can be employed to mitigate some of these ethical concerns.

Ethical Implications of Machine Learning Models

Machine learning models are often perceived as objective, data-driven systems. However, they are far from immune to ethical challenges. Ethical concerns can arise at various stages of the machine learning lifecycle, including data collection, algorithm design, model training, and deployment. These concerns include:

1. Bias in Data

Machine learning models rely heavily on historical data to make predictions. If the data used for training contains biased patterns, the model will likely inherit and propagate these biases. Bias in data can arise from various sources, including historical inequities, biased sampling, or flawed data collection methods. For example, if a recruitment model is trained on a dataset where male candidates were historically preferred, it may continue to prioritize male applicants over female ones, reinforcing existing gender biases.

2. Discrimination and Fairness

Fairness in machine learning refers to the idea that models should treat individuals and groups equally, without discrimination based on characteristics like race, gender, age, or socio-economic status. However, achieving fairness is often complicated. Different fairness metrics can lead to conflicting objectives. For instance, optimizing a model to reduce false negatives for one group may inadvertently increase false positives for another group. Thus, balancing fairness with model performance is a major ethical challenge.

3. Lack of Transparency

Machine learning models, especially complex ones like deep learning, are often regarded as "black boxes" due to their opaque decision-making processes. This lack of transparency can be problematic when models are deployed in high-stakes areas like healthcare, criminal justice, or finance. Stakeholders need to understand how decisions are made, particularly when individuals' lives and opportunities are at stake.

4. Accountability and Responsibility

As machine learning models become more autonomous, determining who is accountable for their outcomes becomes increasingly difficult. For instance, if a loan approval system based on a machine learning model discriminates against a certain demographic group, who should be held responsible? Is it the data scientists who trained the model, the organization that deployed it, or the software developers who built it? Establishing accountability and responsibility is essential for ensuring ethical practices in machine learning.

Bias Detection and Mitigation in Machine Learning

One of the first steps toward building ethical machine learning systems is identifying and mitigating bias. Scikit-Learn, while not explicitly designed for bias detection, provides tools that can be used in the process of auditing models for fairness.

1. Identifying Bias in Data

The first place to check for bias is in the data itself. Before building a machine learning model, it's crucial to assess whether the dataset reflects any biased patterns. Simple statistical techniques, such as comparing the distribution of certain features across demographic groups, can reveal disparities.

For example, in a dataset used for loan approvals, you might check whether the income levels of different racial groups are fairly represented or if certain groups are disproportionately denied loans.

```
import pandas as pd

# Load dataset
data = pd.read_csv('loan_approval.csv')

# Analyze income distribution by race
data.groupby('race')['income'].mean()
```

If significant disparities are found in the income distribution across racial groups, this could be a sign of potential bias in the data that may influence model predictions.

2. Evaluating Model Fairness

Once a model has been trained, fairness can be assessed by examining how it performs across different demographic groups. Scikit-Learn allows you to evaluate model performance using various metrics like accuracy, precision, recall, and F1 scores. By calculating these metrics separately for different groups

241

(e.g., gender or race), you can detect whether the model is biased toward or against any specific group.

```
from sklearn.metrics import precision_score, recall_score

# Generate predictions for the test set
y_pred = model.predict(X_test)

# Evaluate precision and recall for different groups
precision_men = precision_score(y_test_men, y_pred_men)
precision_women = precision_score(y_test_women, y_pred_women)

print("Precision for men:", precision_men)
print("Precision for women:", precision_women)
```

In this example, if the precision for women is significantly lower than for men, it may indicate that the model is biased against female applicants, suggesting the need for further investigation and mitigation.

3. Mitigating Bias with Fairness Constraints

There are several approaches to mitigating bias in machine learning models, including preprocessing the data to remove bias, modifying the algorithm to ensure fairness, and post-processing the model outputs. Although Scikit-Learn does not have built-in fairness

242

constraints, you can apply certain techniques to reduce bias.

a. Re-sampling Techniques: One method for mitigating bias is to re-sample the training data so that underrepresented groups are better represented. You can use techniques like Synthetic Minority Over-sampling (SMOTE) to create synthetic samples for minority groups or undersample the majority class.

```
from imblearn.over_sampling import SMOTE

# Apply SMOTE to balance the dataset
sm = SMOTE(random_state=42)
X_resampled, y_resampled = sm.fit_resample(X_train, y_train)
```

b. Fairness-Aware Algorithms: There are also fairness-aware algorithms, such as fair classifiers, that explicitly incorporate fairness constraints during model training. While Scikit-Learn doesn't include these algorithms by default, third-party libraries like AIF360 from IBM can be integrated with Scikit-Learn to address fairness concerns.

Transparency in Machine Learning Models

Another key ethical consideration is model transparency. As machine learning models become more complex, ensuring interpretability and transparency becomes critical, especially in sensitive applications like healthcare and criminal justice.

1. Explainability with SHAP and LIME

Two popular tools for improving model interpretability are SHAP (SHapley Additive exPlanations) and LIME (Local Interpretable Model-agnostic Explanations). Both tools can be used with Scikit-Learn models to explain individual predictions and provide insights into how models make decisions.

a. SHAP:

SHAP assigns each feature an importance score based on its contribution to the model's prediction. These scores provide a clear understanding of which features drive model decisions.

```python
import shap

# Train a model
model = RandomForestClassifier()
model.fit(X_train, y_train)

# Create a SHAP explainer
explainer = shap.TreeExplainer(model)

# Calculate SHAP values for a specific instance
shap_values = explainer.shap_values(X_test.iloc[0, :])
```

```
# Visualize SHAP values
shap.initjs()
shap.force_plot(explainer.expected_value[1],
shap_values[1], X_test.iloc[0, :])
```

b. LIME:

LIME explains individual predictions by approximating the complex model with a simpler, interpretable model around a specific instance. This allows stakeholders to understand the local behavior of the model, even if the overall model is a "black box."

```
import lime
import lime.lime_tabular

# Initialize a LIME explainer
explainer                                    =
lime.lime_tabular.LimeTabularExplainer(X_train.valu
es, feature_names=X_train.columns)

# Explain a prediction
explanation = explainer.explain_instance(X_test.iloc[0,
:].values, model.predict_proba)
explanation.show_in_notebook()
```

By using these tools, practitioners can ensure that their models are not only accurate but also interpretable, building trust with users and regulators.

Best Practices for Ethical Machine Learning

To mitigate the ethical risks associated with machine learning, organizations and practitioners should adopt best practices, including:

1. Diverse and Inclusive Data Collection

Ensuring that training datasets are representative of the broader population is critical to reducing bias. This means collecting data from diverse sources and ensuring that minority groups are well-represented.

2. Regular Bias Audits

Ethical machine learning should include regular audits to check for bias, discrimination, and unfair outcomes. Audits should be conducted not only during model development but also after deployment to monitor performance over time.

3. Transparent Communication

Machine learning models should come with clear documentation about how they were trained, what data was used, and how predictions are made. Providing this transparency builds trust and ensures accountability.

Machine learning is a powerful tool, but it must be developed and deployed responsibly. Ethical considerations, including bias detection, fairness, and transparency, are critical to ensuring that machine learning models are not only effective but also fair and trustworthy. By leveraging tools like Scikit-Learn, SHAP, and LIME, data scientists can actively work to mitigate ethical concerns and build models that align with societal values and regulations.

Chapter 26

Working with Images: Computer Vision Applications in Scikit-Learn

In recent years, computer vision has emerged as one of the most exciting fields in machine learning, enabling systems to interpret and process visual data. From object detection to facial recognition, image processing applications are rapidly transforming industries. While libraries like TensorFlow and PyTorch are often used for deep learning-based image processing tasks, Scikit-Learn offers robust tools for handling simpler computer vision tasks. This chapter will cover how to preprocess, model, and implement image classification pipelines using Scikit-Learn, and explore tools that integrate computer vision models.

Overview of Image Data in Machine Learning

Images are a unique form of data in machine learning due to their structure. Unlike tabular datasets with distinct features, images consist of pixels arranged in a grid, with each pixel representing intensity or color information. Depending on the complexity of the image, this can create a high-dimensional dataset, requiring specialized preprocessing techniques before applying machine learning models.

Image data typically comes in the form of:

- **Grayscale images**, where each pixel is represented by a single intensity value.
- **RGB images**, where each pixel is represented by three intensity values (Red, Green, and Blue).

Handling these high-dimensional inputs can be challenging, especially for traditional machine learning models, which are better suited for tabular data. However, with the right preprocessing and feature extraction techniques, Scikit-Learn can be used effectively for basic image classification tasks.

Preprocessing Image Data

Preprocessing is a critical step when working with image data. Images need to be resized, normalized, and converted into a format that machine learning algorithms can work with. Scikit-Learn doesn't directly handle raw image data, but by leveraging libraries like NumPy and OpenCV for image manipulation, we can preprocess images before feeding them into Scikit-Learn pipelines.

1. Resizing and Normalizing Images

One of the first steps in image preprocessing is ensuring that all images are of the same size. This is important because machine learning algorithms expect input data to have a uniform shape. You can use libraries like

OpenCV or PIL (Python Imaging Library) to resize images.

```
import cv2

# Load an image using OpenCV
image = cv2.imread('image_path.jpg')

# Resize the image to 64x64 pixels
resized_image = cv2.resize(image, (64, 64))

# Normalize the pixel values to the range [0, 1]
normalized_image = resized_image / 255.0
```

By resizing and normalizing images, you reduce the dimensionality of the dataset, making it easier for machine learning models to process.

2. Flattening Images into Feature Vectors

Traditional machine learning models like decision trees and support vector machines (SVMs) require tabular data, where each row represents a sample and each column represents a feature. For images, you need to flatten the 2D or 3D pixel grids into 1D feature vectors.

```
import numpy as np

# Flatten the image into a 1D vector
flattened_image = normalized_image.flatten()
```

```
# Print the shape of the flattened image
print(flattened_image.shape)
```

For a 64x64 image with three color channels, this flattening process results in a feature vector of length 64 x 64 x 3 = 12,288. This vector represents the pixel intensities of the image, which can be used as input for Scikit-Learn models.

Feature Extraction for Image Data

Directly feeding raw pixel values into machine learning models often leads to poor performance, as these models struggle to capture complex patterns in image data. Feature extraction techniques help simplify the data by transforming images into more meaningful representations. Two common feature extraction techniques are the Histogram of Oriented Gradients (HOG) and Scale-Invariant Feature Transform (SIFT).

1. Histogram of Oriented Gradients (HOG)

HOG is a popular feature extraction technique for images. It works by computing the gradient orientation of pixels, capturing edge structures in an image, which are critical for identifying objects.

```
from skimage.feature import hog
from skimage import data, exposure

# Compute HOG features and visualize the results
```

251

```
fd, hog_image = hog(resized_image, orientations=9,
pixels_per_cell=(8, 8),
              cells_per_block=(2, 2), visualize=True,
multichannel=True)
```

```
# Adjust the image for better contrast
hog_image_rescaled                          =
exposure.rescale_intensity(hog_image,    in_range=(0,
10))
```

The HOG feature vector is much smaller than the raw pixel data and encodes important information about the structure of objects in the image.

2. Scale-Invariant Feature Transform (SIFT)

SIFT is another powerful feature extraction technique, particularly useful for matching key points between images. While not directly available in Scikit-Learn, SIFT can be used alongside Scikit-Learn pipelines.

```
import cv2
```

```
# Convert the image to grayscale
gray_image       =       cv2.cvtColor(resized_image,
cv2.COLOR_BGR2GRAY)
```

```
# Detect keypoints and compute descriptors using SIFT
sift = cv2.SIFT_create()
```

```
keypoints,              descriptors       =
sift.detectAndCompute(gray_image, None)

# Draw keypoints on the image
image_with_keypoints                      =
cv2.drawKeypoints(resized_image, keypoints, None)
```

By applying SIFT, you extract unique features from the image that are invariant to scaling, rotation, and translation, making them useful for object recognition tasks.

Image Classification Using Scikit-Learn

Once the images are preprocessed and feature vectors are extracted, you can use Scikit-Learn's powerful classification algorithms to build models for image classification tasks. For this chapter, we will focus on using a simple pipeline with a support vector machine (SVM) for image classification.

1. Building an Image Classification Pipeline

The following example demonstrates how to build an image classification pipeline in Scikit-Learn using HOG features and an SVM classifier:

```
from sklearn.svm import SVC
from sklearn.pipeline import Pipeline
from sklearn.preprocessing import StandardScaler
from sklearn.model_selection import train_test_split
```

```python
from sklearn.metrics import accuracy_score

# Example dataset of flattened images and labels
X = [flatten_image(img) for img in images]  # Flatten
all images
y = labels  # Corresponding labels

# Split the dataset into training and testing sets
X_train, X_test, y_train, y_test = train_test_split(X, y,
test_size=0.2, random_state=42)

# Create a pipeline with scaling and SVM
pipeline = Pipeline([
    ('scaler', StandardScaler()),
    ('classifier', SVC(kernel='linear'))
])

# Train the model
pipeline.fit(X_train, y_train)

# Make predictions and evaluate the model
y_pred = pipeline.predict(X_test)
print("Accuracy:", accuracy_score(y_test, y_pred))
```

By combining image preprocessing, feature extraction, and classification into a single pipeline, Scikit-Learn simplifies the process of building machine learning models for image classification.

Integrating Deep Learning for Complex Image Tasks

While Scikit-Learn provides tools for basic image classification, deep learning is often more effective for complex computer vision tasks. Fortunately, you can integrate Scikit-Learn with deep learning frameworks like TensorFlow to take advantage of the power of neural networks for image classification.

1. Using TensorFlow for Image Classification

For more advanced image classification tasks, you can use pre-trained deep learning models like convolutional neural networks (CNNs). TensorFlow's Keras API provides simple tools to load and fine-tune these models.

```python
import tensorflow as tf
from tensorflow.keras.applications import VGG16
from tensorflow.keras.preprocessing.image import ImageDataGenerator

# Load a pre-trained VGG16 model
model = VGG16(weights='imagenet', include_top=False, input_shape=(64, 64, 3))

# Freeze the layers of the model
for layer in model.layers:
    layer.trainable = False
```

```
# Add custom layers for classification
x = tf.keras.layers.Flatten()(model.output)
x = tf.keras.layers.Dense(256, activation='relu')(x)
x = tf.keras.layers.Dense(10, activation='softmax')(x)

# Create a new model
custom_model                                        =
tf.keras.models.Model(inputs=model.input, outputs=x)

# Compile and train the model
custom_model.compile(optimizer='adam',
loss='categorical_crossentropy', metrics=['accuracy'])

# Image data generator for augmentation
datagen     =     ImageDataGenerator(rescale=1./255,
rotation_range=20,              width_shift_range=0.2,
height_shift_range=0.2)

# Train the model
custom_model.fit(datagen.flow(X_train,      y_train),
epochs=10)
```

This workflow allows you to combine Scikit-Learn's data processing and model evaluation tools with the power of deep learning for complex computer vision tasks.

While Scikit-Learn may not be the first choice for advanced image processing tasks, it remains a versatile tool for building basic computer vision models. Through careful preprocessing and feature extraction, traditional machine learning algorithms like SVMs can be used effectively for image classification. For more complex tasks, Scikit-Learn's integration with deep learning frameworks like TensorFlow provides a powerful solution, enabling you to harness the strengths of both machine learning approaches.

Chapter 27

Building Robust Scikit-Learn Models with Imputation Techniques

Handling missing data is one of the most critical challenges in machine learning workflows, particularly when working with real-world datasets. Missing values can occur due to various reasons, such as data corruption, errors in data collection, or simply unavailable information. If left untreated, these gaps can severely impact the performance of machine learning models, as most algorithms in Scikit-Learn do not handle missing data natively.

Imputation techniques fill in these missing values in a way that maintains the integrity of the dataset and ensures the model performs effectively. This chapter will explore various imputation techniques, from basic methods like mean and median imputation to more advanced approaches like iterative imputation and matrix factorization, and how to implement them using Scikit-Learn.

The Impact of Missing Data on Machine Learning Models

Missing data poses multiple challenges in machine learning. For instance, training a model on incomplete data may result in biased or inaccurate predictions. If a significant portion of the data is missing, dropping rows or columns with missing values may lead to the loss of valuable information. As a result, effective handling of missing data through imputation is essential for building robust models.

There are three types of missing data:

- **Missing Completely at Random (MCAR):** The missing values are independent of both observed and unobserved data.
- **Missing at Random (MAR):** The missing values are related to other observed variables but not to the missing variable itself.
- **Missing Not at Random (MNAR):** The missing values depend on unobserved variables or the values that are missing.

Understanding the nature of the missing data is crucial for selecting the appropriate imputation technique.

Basic Imputation Techniques in Scikit-Learn

Scikit-Learn provides simple yet effective imputation techniques that are suitable for datasets with minimal missing data or cases where data is missing completely at random.

1. Mean, Median, and Mode Imputation

The most straightforward approach to imputation is to fill missing values with the mean, median, or mode of the feature. While this method is fast and easy to implement, it assumes that the data distribution is uniform and may introduce bias, especially for features with outliers or skewed distributions.

```
from sklearn.impute import SimpleImputer

# Create an imputer object with the mean strategy
imputer = SimpleImputer(strategy='mean')

# Fit the imputer to the dataset and transform it
X_imputed = imputer.fit_transform(X)
```

For numerical features, the mean and median are commonly used, while for categorical features, mode imputation (filling with the most frequent category) is preferred.

```
# Mode imputation for categorical variables
imputer = SimpleImputer(strategy='most_frequent')
X_imputed = imputer.fit_transform(X)
```

Although these methods are widely used, they can fail to capture the underlying structure of the data, particularly when missing values are not missing completely at random.

Advanced Imputation Techniques

When dealing with large datasets or cases where missing values are related to other features, more sophisticated imputation techniques should be used. These methods aim to leverage the relationships between features to impute missing values in a way that reflects the data's inherent structure.

1. K-Nearest Neighbors (KNN) Imputation

KNN imputation is a distance-based method that fills missing values using the k-nearest neighbors of each sample. The idea is to find samples in the dataset that are most similar to the sample with missing values and use their values to impute the missing ones. This method works well when there is a strong correlation between features.

```
from sklearn.impute import KNNImputer

# Create a KNN imputer object with 5 neighbors
knn_imputer = KNNImputer(n_neighbors=5)

# Fit and transform the dataset
X_imputed = knn_imputer.fit_transform(X)
```

KNN imputation is more effective than mean or median imputation, as it uses the structure of the data to infer missing values. However, it can be computationally expensive, especially for large datasets.

2. Iterative Imputation

Iterative imputation is an advanced method that models each feature with missing values as a function of the other features. It performs multiple iterations, using the predictions from the previous iteration to impute the missing values. Scikit-Learn provides the IterativeImputer class, which implements a method similar to the Multivariate Imputation by Chained Equations (MICE) algorithm.

```
from sklearn.experimental import enable_iterative_imputer
from sklearn.impute import IterativeImputer

# Create an iterative imputer object
iterative_imputer = IterativeImputer()

# Fit and transform the dataset
X_imputed = iterative_imputer.fit_transform(X)
```

This method is particularly useful when features are highly correlated, as it takes into account the relationships between variables. Iterative imputation typically results in more accurate imputations compared to simpler methods like mean or KNN imputation.

3. Matrix Factorization for Imputation

Matrix factorization is a powerful technique for imputation, particularly in the context of collaborative filtering and recommender systems. The idea is to decompose the dataset into two matrices, with one matrix representing latent features and the other representing feature interactions. Missing values can then be filled by approximating them based on these latent factors.

In machine learning, matrix factorization is commonly used in combination with Singular Value Decomposition (SVD) or non-negative matrix factorization (NMF).

```python
from sklearn.decomposition import TruncatedSVD
import numpy as np

# Replace missing values with the mean as an initial step
X_filled = np.where(np.isnan(X), np.nanmean(X, axis=0), X)

# Apply matrix factorization
svd = TruncatedSVD(n_components=10)
X_imputed = svd.fit_transform(X_filled)
```

While Scikit-Learn does not provide direct support for matrix factorization-based imputation, the technique can be implemented manually or through other specialized libraries like fancyimpute.

Choosing the Right Imputation Technique

Selecting the appropriate imputation technique depends on several factors, including the size of the dataset, the proportion of missing values, the relationship between features, and the type of data (numerical or categorical). Below are some general guidelines for choosing the right method:

- **Mean, median, and mode imputation**: Use when the dataset is small, and the missing data is completely at random.
- **KNN imputation**: Use when the dataset has a moderate number of missing values, and features are correlated.
- **Iterative imputation**: Use when features are highly correlated, and the dataset is large or complex.
- **Matrix factorization**: Use in recommender systems or datasets where missing values can be predicted based on latent factors.

Evaluating the Effectiveness of Imputation

Once missing values are imputed, it's essential to assess the impact of the imputation technique on model performance. One common approach is to evaluate the performance of a machine learning model before and after imputation to determine how well the imputation method works. Cross-validation can be helpful in this regard.

```
from sklearn.model_selection import cross_val_score
```

```python
from sklearn.ensemble import RandomForestClassifier

# Train a random forest classifier on the imputed dataset
model = RandomForestClassifier()

# Perform cross-validation
scores = cross_val_score(model, X_imputed, y, cv=5)

print("Cross-validation accuracy: ", scores.mean())
```

By comparing the performance of different imputation techniques, you can determine which method results in the best model performance for your specific dataset.

Imputation in Pipelines

In practice, it's often useful to include the imputation process in a Scikit-Learn pipeline. This allows you to automate the preprocessing steps and ensure that the same imputation method is applied to both the training and testing datasets.

```python
from sklearn.pipeline import Pipeline

# Create a pipeline with iterative imputation and a
random forest classifier
pipeline = Pipeline([
    ('imputer', IterativeImputer()),
    ('classifier', RandomForestClassifier())
])
```

```
# Train and evaluate the model
pipeline.fit(X_train, y_train)
accuracy = pipeline.score(X_test, y_test)
print("Model accuracy after imputation: ", accuracy)
```

By incorporating imputation into a pipeline, you can streamline your machine learning workflow and build robust models that handle missing data effectively.

Imputation is a crucial step in the machine learning pipeline, especially when dealing with real-world datasets that often contain missing values. While simple imputation methods like mean or median can be effective for small datasets, more advanced techniques like KNN, iterative imputation, and matrix factorization are better suited for handling complex datasets with missing data. By using Scikit-Learn's imputation tools, you can build more robust models that maintain their performance even in the presence of incomplete data. Incorporating these imputation techniques into your machine learning pipeline ensures that your models are both accurate and reliable, regardless of missing values.

Chapter 28

Model Validation: Avoiding Overfitting and Underfitting

Building machine learning models that generalize well to unseen data is a delicate balancing act. Two common pitfalls in this process are **overfitting** and **underfitting**. Overfitting occurs when a model is too complex and captures noise in the training data, leading to poor generalization on new data. Underfitting, on the other hand, happens when a model is too simple, failing to capture the underlying structure of the data, resulting in low accuracy on both the training and testing datasets.

This chapter explores various techniques to avoid both overfitting and underfitting, such as **regularization**, **dropout**, and **early stopping**. These methods help strike the right balance between model complexity and performance, allowing for better generalization and more accurate predictions.

Understanding Overfitting and Underfitting

Before delving into techniques to address these issues, it's important to understand their core characteristics and how they manifest in machine learning models.

- **Overfitting**: This occurs when the model performs exceptionally well on the training data but poorly on unseen test data. Overfitting happens when the model memorizes the training data, including its noise and outliers, instead of learning the general patterns. As a result, the model struggles to generalize to new examples.

Common signs of overfitting:

- High accuracy on the training set but low accuracy on the validation or test set.
- A large gap between the training and test performance.
- **Underfitting**: Underfitting happens when a model is too simplistic and cannot capture the underlying patterns in the data. In this case, the model performs poorly on both the training and test datasets, indicating that it fails to model the data adequately.

Common signs of underfitting:

- Low accuracy on both the training and test sets.
- A small gap between training and test performance, with both showing poor results.

Techniques to Avoid Overfitting

Several techniques can be employed to mitigate overfitting, ensuring that the model generalizes well to new data without memorizing the noise in the training data.

1. Regularization

Regularization is a technique that penalizes model complexity by adding a regularization term to the loss function. This term discourages the model from relying too heavily on certain features or fitting noise. Scikit-Learn offers two primary types of regularization for linear models: **L1 (Lasso) Regularization** and **L2 (Ridge) Regularization**.

- **L1 Regularization (Lasso)**: L1 regularization penalizes the absolute values of the model's coefficients, which can result in some coefficients becoming zero. This makes L1 regularization useful for feature selection, as it can completely eliminate irrelevant features.

```
from sklearn.linear_model import Lasso

# Lasso regression with regularization strength (alpha)
lasso = Lasso(alpha=0.1)
lasso.fit(X_train, y_train)

# Model performance
train_score = lasso.score(X_train, y_train)
test_score = lasso.score(X_test, y_test)
```

- **L2 Regularization (Ridge)**: L2 regularization penalizes the square of the coefficients, shrinking them toward zero but not completely eliminating any. This technique is useful for reducing the variance of the model without fully discarding features.

```
from sklearn.linear_model import Ridge
```

```
# Ridge regression with regularization strength (alpha)
ridge = Ridge(alpha=1.0)
ridge.fit(X_train, y_train)

# Model performance
train_score = ridge.score(X_train, y_train)
test_score = ridge.score(X_test, y_test)
```

In both cases, the strength of the regularization is controlled by the hyperparameter alpha, which can be fine-tuned using cross-validation.

2. Dropout (for Neural Networks)

Dropout is a regularization technique primarily used in neural networks to prevent overfitting. It works by randomly "dropping out" a subset of neurons during training, forcing the network to learn redundant representations. This prevents the network from becoming too reliant on specific neurons, leading to a more generalized model.

While dropout is not natively supported in Scikit-Learn, it can be implemented when integrating Scikit-Learn with TensorFlow or Keras for deep learning models.

```
from tensorflow.keras.layers import Dropout
from tensorflow.keras.models import Sequential
from tensorflow.keras.layers import Dense

# Neural network with dropout
```

```python
model = Sequential([
    Dense(128,                          activation='relu',
input_shape=(input_dim,)),
    Dropout(0.5),  # Dropout layer with a 50% dropout
rate
    Dense(64, activation='relu'),
    Dropout(0.5),
    Dense(1, activation='sigmoid')
])

model.compile(optimizer='adam',
loss='binary_crossentropy', metrics=['accuracy'])
```

3. Early Stopping

Early stopping is a technique that monitors the model's performance on the validation dataset during training and stops the training process once the validation performance stops improving. This prevents the model from overfitting by halting training before it begins to memorize the noise in the data.

Early stopping is commonly used in neural networks but can also be applied to boosting algorithms like XGBoost, which allow for monitoring validation performance during training.

```python
from tensorflow.keras.callbacks import EarlyStopping

# Early stopping with a patience of 5 epochs
```

271

```
early_stopping  =  EarlyStopping(monitor='val_loss',
patience=5, restore_best_weights=True)
```

```
# Train the model with early stopping
model.fit(X_train, y_train, validation_data=(X_val,
y_val), epochs=100, callbacks=[early_stopping])
```

By stopping training early, you can avoid overfitting while still ensuring that the model captures meaningful patterns in the data.

4. Cross-Validation

Cross-validation is an essential technique for model validation that helps prevent overfitting. By splitting the data into multiple subsets and training the model on different splits, cross-validation provides a more robust estimate of model performance. **k-fold cross-validation** is the most commonly used approach, where the dataset is divided into k subsets, and the model is trained on k-1 subsets and tested on the remaining subset. This process is repeated k times, with each subset serving as the test set once.

```
from sklearn.model_selection import cross_val_score
from sklearn.ensemble import RandomForestClassifier
```

```
# Perform 5-fold cross-validation
model = RandomForestClassifier()
scores = cross_val_score(model, X, y, cv=5)
```

```
print("Cross-validation scores: ", scores)
```

Cross-validation helps ensure that the model performs well across different subsets of data, reducing the risk of overfitting.

Techniques to Avoid Underfitting

While overfitting is more common in complex models, underfitting can also pose a significant problem, particularly when the model is too simplistic. Below are some techniques to avoid underfitting and improve model performance.

1. Increase Model Complexity

If a model is underfitting, it may be too simple to capture the complexity of the data. In such cases, increasing the complexity of the model can help improve its performance. For example, in a decision tree model, you can increase the depth of the tree to allow for more complex decision boundaries.

```
from sklearn.tree import DecisionTreeClassifier

# Increase tree depth to reduce underfitting
model = DecisionTreeClassifier(max_depth=10)
model.fit(X_train, y_train)
```

Similarly, in neural networks, adding more layers or neurons can make the model more expressive, allowing it to capture intricate patterns in the data.

2. Remove Regularization

While regularization helps prevent overfitting, using too much regularization can lead to underfitting. If your model is underfitting, reducing or removing regularization may improve its performance.

```
# Reduce regularization strength
ridge = Ridge(alpha=0.01)
ridge.fit(X_train, y_train)
```

3. Feature Engineering and Selection

Underfitting can also occur when the model lacks sufficient information to make accurate predictions. In such cases, feature engineering—creating new features or transforming existing ones—can help the model capture more relevant patterns. Feature selection techniques, such as Recursive Feature Elimination (RFE), can also improve model performance by identifying the most important features.

```
from sklearn.feature_selection import RFE
from sklearn.linear_model import LogisticRegression

# Recursive Feature Elimination (RFE) for feature selection
```

```
model = LogisticRegression()
rfe = RFE(model, n_features_to_select=10)
X_selected = rfe.fit_transform(X, y)
```

Balancing Model Complexity and Accuracy

Achieving the right balance between overfitting and underfitting is crucial for building machine learning models that generalize well to unseen data. Here are some strategies for finding this balance:

- **Hyperparameter Tuning**: Use techniques like **grid search** and **random search** to tune hyperparameters and find the optimal settings that prevent both overfitting and underfitting.

```
from sklearn.model_selection import GridSearchCV

# Grid search for hyperparameter tuning
param_grid = {'alpha': [0.01, 0.1, 1.0]}
grid_search = GridSearchCV(Ridge(), param_grid,
cv=5)
grid_search.fit(X_train, y_train)

print("Best parameters: ", grid_search.best_params_)
```

- **Cross-Validation**: Cross-validation provides an unbiased estimate of model performance on unseen data, helping to identify whether the model is overfitting or underfitting.

- **Regularization and Early Stopping**: Techniques like regularization and early stopping can help fine-tune the model's complexity, preventing it from being too simple or too complex.

By leveraging these strategies, you can develop models that avoid overfitting and underfitting, ensuring that they perform well on both the training and test datasets.

Chapter 29

Scaling Machine Learning with Cloud Platforms

As the volume of data grows and machine learning models become more complex, there is an increasing demand for computational resources that can handle large-scale training and inference tasks. While local machines may be sufficient for small to moderately-sized datasets, scaling machine learning workflows often requires the power of cloud platforms. These platforms offer scalable computing resources, including distributed systems, specialized hardware like GPUs and TPUs, and robust storage solutions, enabling the efficient training of large models on vast datasets.

In this chapter, we will explore how to integrate Scikit-Learn with popular cloud platforms such as **Amazon Web Services (AWS)**, **Google Cloud Platform (GCP)**, and **Microsoft Azure**. We will also look at how to utilize cloud-based infrastructure for training machine learning models at scale, focusing on the efficient use of cloud computing resources to streamline machine learning workflows.

Why Use Cloud Platforms for Machine Learning?

Cloud platforms provide several advantages when scaling machine learning tasks. These benefits are particularly evident when working with large datasets, complex models, or real-time applications.

1. **Scalability**: Cloud platforms offer the ability to easily scale computing resources up or down based on demand. This flexibility is particularly useful when training deep learning models or working with large datasets that require extensive computational power.
2. **Cost-Effectiveness**: Instead of investing in expensive hardware, cloud platforms allow you to pay for only the computing resources you need. You can rent cloud instances with specific configurations (CPU, GPU, memory) and release them after completing your tasks, saving costs on infrastructure maintenance.
3. **Access to Specialized Hardware**: Training large machine learning models often requires GPUs or TPUs to accelerate computations. Cloud platforms provide access to these specialized hardware options, making it easier to build and train high-performance models without having to invest in physical hardware.
4. **Collaboration and Flexibility**: Cloud-based machine learning environments can be easily shared with team members across different locations, enabling seamless collaboration on model development, training, and deployment.
5. **Pre-Built Machine Learning Services**: Many cloud platforms offer pre-built machine learning services and frameworks, enabling quick deployment and experimentation without the need for building models

from scratch. Scikit-Learn can be integrated with these services to handle various machine learning tasks more efficiently.

Integrating Scikit-Learn with AWS

Amazon Web Services (AWS) is one of the most popular cloud platforms for machine learning, offering a wide range of services and tools for training and deploying models. Scikit-Learn can be integrated with several AWS services, including **Amazon SageMaker** for large-scale training, **AWS Lambda** for serverless computing, and **Elastic Beanstalk** for model deployment.

1. Using Amazon SageMaker with Scikit-Learn

Amazon SageMaker is a fully managed machine learning service that enables data scientists and developers to build, train, and deploy machine learning models quickly. SageMaker supports multiple machine learning frameworks, including Scikit-Learn, TensorFlow, and PyTorch.

To get started with SageMaker, you can use the **SageMaker Scikit-Learn container**, which provides a pre-configured environment for running Scikit-Learn models. You can also bring your own custom Scikit-Learn scripts and run them in the cloud using the SageMaker platform.

```python
import sagemaker
from sagemaker.sklearn import SKLearn

# Define a SageMaker session
sagemaker_session = sagemaker.Session()

# S3 bucket to store input/output data
bucket = 'my-sagemaker-bucket'

# Path to the Scikit-Learn training script
entry_point = 'train.py'

# Create an estimator for the Scikit-Learn model
sklearn_estimator = SKLearn(entry_point=entry_point,
                role='my-aws-role',
                framework_version='0.23-1',
                instance_count=1,
                instance_type='ml.m5.large',
                output_path=f's3://{bucket}/output',

sagemaker_session=sagemaker_session)

# Fit the estimator with data in S3
sklearn_estimator.fit({'train':
f's3://{bucket}/data/train.csv'})
```

Using SageMaker, you can train your Scikit-Learn models on large datasets using powerful cloud resources and easily deploy the models for real-time inference.

2. Using AWS Lambda for Serverless Model Deployment

AWS Lambda is a serverless computing service that enables you to run code without provisioning or managing servers. You can use AWS Lambda to deploy Scikit-Learn models as serverless applications, allowing for highly scalable, low-latency machine learning inferences.

Here's how you can deploy a Scikit-Learn model using AWS Lambda:

- First, train the model locally or on an AWS EC2 instance, then serialize it using **Joblib** or **Pickle**.
- Upload the serialized model to an S3 bucket.
- Create a Lambda function that loads the model from S3 and performs inference on incoming requests.

```python
import joblib
import boto3

def lambda_handler(event, context):
    # Load the Scikit-Learn model from S3
    s3 = boto3.client('s3')
    s3.download_file('my-s3-bucket', 'my-model.joblib', '/tmp/my-model.joblib')

    model = joblib.load('/tmp/my-model.joblib')

    # Perform inference
```

```
input_data = event['data']
prediction = model.predict(input_data)

return {'prediction': prediction}
```

With AWS Lambda, you can deploy Scikit-Learn models with ease, scaling automatically to handle large numbers of requests without managing any infrastructure.

Integrating Scikit-Learn with Google Cloud Platform (GCP)

Google Cloud Platform (GCP) offers a comprehensive suite of tools and services for machine learning. GCP's **AI Platform** provides scalable infrastructure for training and deploying models, while **BigQuery** allows you to analyze large datasets efficiently.

1. Using AI Platform with Scikit-Learn

Google's **AI Platform** enables you to train and deploy machine learning models in a fully managed environment. AI Platform supports custom Scikit-Learn models, allowing you to train large-scale models on GCP infrastructure.

To train a Scikit-Learn model using AI Platform, you can package your training code into a Python module and submit a training job using the gcloud command-line tool.

```
gcloud ai-platform jobs submit training my_job \
  --module-name=trainer.task \
  --package-path=./trainer \
  --region=us-central1 \
  --python-version=3.7 \
  --runtime-version=2.3 \
  --scale-tier=BASIC_GPU \
  --job-dir=gs://my-bucket/job-dir
```

After training, you can deploy your model as a REST API using AI Platform's prediction service.

2. Using BigQuery for Data Processing

BigQuery is Google's fully managed data warehouse that supports SQL queries on massive datasets. Scikit-Learn models can be integrated with BigQuery for efficient data preprocessing and feature extraction.

Using the google-cloud-bigquery library, you can directly query BigQuery tables and load the data into a Pandas DataFrame, which can then be used with Scikit-Learn for model training.

```
from google.cloud import bigquery
import pandas as pd
```

```python
# Initialize BigQuery client
client = bigquery.Client()

# Query data from BigQuery
query = "SELECT * FROM `my-dataset.my-table`"
df = client.query(query).to_dataframe()

# Use the data with Scikit-Learn
from sklearn.ensemble import RandomForestClassifier

X = df.drop(columns=['target'])
y = df['target']

model = RandomForestClassifier()
model.fit(X, y)
```

Integrating Scikit-Learn with Microsoft Azure

Microsoft Azure offers **Azure Machine Learning (Azure ML)**, a fully managed service that supports end-to-end machine learning workflows. Azure ML integrates seamlessly with Scikit-Learn, allowing you to train and deploy models at scale.

1. Using Azure ML for Scikit-Learn

With Azure ML, you can create and manage machine learning environments, run training jobs on cloud compute instances, and deploy models for inference. To train a Scikit-Learn model on Azure ML, you can create an Azure ML workspace and submit a training job using the azureml-sdk.

```
from azureml.core import Workspace, Experiment,
ScriptRunConfig
from azureml.core.environment import Environment

# Initialize workspace
ws = Workspace.from_config()

# Create an experiment
experiment = Experiment(workspace=ws, name='my-experiment')

# Define a Scikit-Learn environment
sklearn_env                                =
Environment.from_conda_specification(name='sklearn
-env', file_path='environment.yml')

# Define a script configuration for training
src      =      ScriptRunConfig(source_directory='./src',
script='train.py', environment=sklearn_env)

# Submit the training job
run = experiment.submit(src)
run.wait_for_completion()
```

2. Using Azure Databricks for Large-Scale Training

Azure also integrates with **Databricks**, a cloud platform optimized for big data analytics. Databricks offers an interactive environment for running Apache Spark and allows you to scale Scikit-Learn workflows using distributed computing. You can use libraries like **Koalas** or **MLlib** to scale Scikit-Learn-style workflows on Spark clusters.

```
import databricks.koalas as ks
from sklearn.ensemble import GradientBoostingClassifier

# Load data into Koalas DataFrame (compatible with Pandas API)
df = ks.read_csv('dbfs:/mnt/my-bucket/data.csv')

# Train Scikit-Learn model on Databricks cluster
X = df.drop(columns=['target']).to_pandas()
y = df['target'].to_pandas()

model = GradientBoostingClassifier()
model.fit(X, y)
```

Challenges of Scaling Machine Learning in the Cloud

While cloud platforms provide immense power and flexibility, they also introduce several challenges that you need to address when scaling machine learning workflows.

286

1. **Data Transfer Costs**: Moving large datasets to and from the cloud can incur significant costs, especially when dealing with terabytes of data. It's important to minimize data transfer and use cloud-native storage solutions like S3, BigQuery, or Azure Blob Storage.
2. **Model Latency**: While cloud resources can scale to handle large datasets, the latency of model predictions can be a bottleneck in real-time applications. To reduce latency, use edge computing or cache frequently used models.
3. **Security and Privacy**: When working with sensitive data, it's crucial to ensure that the cloud platform complies with security and privacy regulations. Services like AWS, GCP, and Azure provide tools for encryption, access control, and audit logging, but you need to configure them properly.
4. **Resource Management**: Managing cloud resources can be complex, especially when working with distributed systems. It's important to monitor resource usage closely and terminate idle instances to avoid unexpected costs.

Cloud platforms have revolutionized how machine learning models are built, trained, and deployed at scale. By leveraging services like AWS, GCP, and Azure, you can access powerful computing resources, scale your machine learning workflows, and reduce the time it takes to bring models to production. Integrating Scikit-Learn with cloud platforms allows you to take full advantage of cloud-based infrastructure, ensuring that your models can handle even the most demanding tasks efficiently and cost-effectively.

Chapter 30

Exploratory Data Analysis with Scikit-Learn

Before diving into model building and machine learning, it is crucial to understand the underlying structure, patterns, and relationships in the dataset. This process, known as **Exploratory Data Analysis (EDA)**, helps uncover hidden trends, detect anomalies, and set the foundation for successful model development. EDA involves a mix of **data visualizations**, **statistical summaries**, and **feature analysis** to gain insights that guide feature engineering and model selection.

While Scikit-Learn is primarily known for its machine learning algorithms, it also provides several useful tools for EDA. These tools can be combined with other libraries like **Pandas**, **Matplotlib**, and **Seaborn** to form a comprehensive framework for understanding your data. In this chapter, we'll explore various EDA techniques using Scikit-Learn, and how these insights can shape the machine learning process.

The Role of Exploratory Data Analysis in Machine Learning

EDA serves as the initial phase of any data science or machine learning project. Its goal is to explore the dataset by identifying important variables, patterns, and potential challenges such as missing data or outliers. A strong understanding of the dataset before running algorithms improves model accuracy, prevents overfitting, and reduces model bias.

The primary objectives of EDA are:

1. **Summarize the dataset**: EDA provides a statistical summary of the dataset, including central tendencies like the mean, median, and standard deviation, as well as distributions, correlations, and missing values.
2. **Visualize data relationships**: Visual tools like histograms, scatter plots, and correlation heatmaps reveal underlying patterns and trends that might not be apparent in numerical summaries alone.
3. **Detect anomalies**: EDA helps identify outliers, unusual patterns, and missing data that could affect model performance.
4. **Guide feature selection**: Understanding the relationships between features and target variables helps you select which features to include in the machine learning model.
5. **Hypothesis testing**: EDA allows you to test preliminary hypotheses about the data and gain deeper insights into its structure.

Loading and Preparing Data for EDA with Scikit-Learn

The first step in EDA is loading and inspecting the dataset. Scikit-Learn provides utilities for loading sample datasets such as **Iris**, **Wine**, and **Diabetes**, which can be used to practice EDA techniques. Additionally, Scikit-Learn supports integration with Pandas DataFrames, allowing you to perform data manipulation and analysis with ease.

```python
from sklearn.datasets import load_iris
import pandas as pd

# Load the Iris dataset
iris = load_iris()

# Create a DataFrame from the dataset
df = pd.DataFrame(data=iris.data,
columns=iris.feature_names)
df['target'] = iris.target

# Display the first few rows
print(df.head())
```

In the example above, we load the Iris dataset, convert it into a Pandas DataFrame, and inspect the first few rows. The target column represents the class labels, while the remaining columns represent the features of the dataset.

Summarizing the Dataset with Descriptive Statistics

Understanding basic statistics about your data is one of the first steps in EDA. Scikit-Learn's integration with

Pandas allows you to quickly generate descriptive statistics for each feature in the dataset, including measures of central tendency, spread, and distribution.

```
# Descriptive statistics for the features
summary = df.describe()
print(summary)
```

The .describe() function generates a summary of the dataset, showing key metrics such as:

- **Count**: The number of non-null entries in each column.
- **Mean**: The average value of each feature.
- **Standard Deviation**: The amount of variation or dispersion in each feature.
- **Min and Max**: The minimum and maximum values in each column.
- **Percentiles (25th, 50th, 75th)**: Values below which a given percentage of data points fall, helping to understand the distribution shape.

Handling Missing Data

Missing data can pose significant challenges for machine learning algorithms. It's essential to identify and handle missing values during EDA. Scikit-Learn provides imputation techniques that allow you to replace missing values with meaningful substitutes.

First, let's check for missing values:

```
# Check for missing values
missing_values = df.isnull().sum()
print(missing_values)
```

If missing values are detected, you can use Scikit-Learn's **SimpleImputer** to fill them:

```
from sklearn.impute import SimpleImputer

# Create an imputer object with a strategy for filling
missing values
imputer = SimpleImputer(strategy='mean')

# Fit and transform the data to fill missing values
df_filled = pd.DataFrame(imputer.fit_transform(df),
columns=df.columns)
```

The **SimpleImputer** replaces missing values with the mean (or another statistic, like median or mode) of the respective feature, ensuring that your dataset is complete before feeding it into a machine learning model.

Data Visualization Techniques for EDA

Visualizations play a vital role in EDA by helping you see patterns and relationships that are not obvious from raw data. Scikit-Learn, in combination with libraries like **Matplotlib** and **Seaborn**, can be used to generate meaningful visualizations that highlight trends, distributions, and outliers.

1. Histograms

Histograms provide a way to visualize the distribution of individual features. They show the frequency of data points across different bins and can help detect skewness in the data.

```
import matplotlib.pyplot as plt

# Plot histograms for each feature
df.hist(bins=20, figsize=(10, 8))
plt.show()
```

Histograms are particularly useful for identifying whether the data follows a normal distribution, whether there are outliers, and whether certain features need transformation.

2. Scatter Plots

Scatter plots visualize the relationship between two features, making it easy to identify correlations, clusters, or outliers.

```
# Scatter plot of two features
plt.scatter(df['sepal length (cm)'], df['sepal width (cm)'],
c=df['target'])
plt.xlabel('Sepal Length (cm)')
```

```python
plt.ylabel('Sepal Width (cm)')
plt.title('Scatter Plot of Sepal Length vs. Width')
plt.show()
```

By using color to represent different target classes (as shown above), scatter plots can reveal how features separate different categories of data.

3. Correlation Heatmaps

Correlation matrices are used to calculate the linear relationship between numerical features. Heatmaps visually represent these correlations, allowing you to easily spot highly correlated features.

```python
import seaborn as sns

# Compute the correlation matrix
correlation_matrix = df.corr()

# Plot a heatmap of the correlation matrix
sns.heatmap(correlation_matrix,        annot=True,
cmap='coolwarm')
plt.title('Feature Correlation Matrix')
plt.show()
```

Highly correlated features can indicate multicollinearity, which may reduce the predictive power of a machine learning model. If two features are highly correlated, you might consider removing one of them to simplify the model.

Feature Engineering: Preparing Data for Modeling

EDA is closely linked with **feature engineering**, the process of selecting, transforming, and creating new features that improve model performance. During EDA, you can identify important features and create new ones that might enhance your model's predictive accuracy.

1. Feature Scaling

Machine learning algorithms like linear regression, k-nearest neighbors, and support vector machines require that features be on the same scale. You can use Scikit-Learn's StandardScaler or MinMaxScaler to normalize or standardize your features.

```
from sklearn.preprocessing import StandardScaler

# Create a scaler object
scaler = StandardScaler()

# Scale the features
df_scaled                                    =
pd.DataFrame(scaler.fit_transform(df.drop(columns='t
arget')), columns=df.columns[:-1])
```

2. Feature Selection

Feature selection is the process of selecting the most important features for model building. By understanding the relationships between the target variable and the features during EDA, you can decide which features to include or exclude.

Scikit-Learn offers several feature selection techniques, such as **SelectKBest** and **Recursive Feature Elimination (RFE)**, that allow you to choose features based on their importance.

```python
from sklearn.feature_selection import SelectKBest, f_classif

# Select the top 2 features based on ANOVA F-value
selector = SelectKBest(score_func=f_classif, k=2)
selected_features = selector.fit_transform(df.drop(columns='target'), df['target'])

print("Selected Features:\n", selected_features)
```

Analyzing Target Distribution

In classification tasks, it is important to understand the distribution of the target variable. If the target classes are imbalanced (i.e., some classes are much more frequent than others), this can lead to poor model performance. Analyzing the target distribution during EDA helps you decide whether you need to apply techniques like oversampling or undersampling to balance the dataset.

```
# Plot the distribution of the target variable
df['target'].value_counts().plot(kind='bar')
plt.title('Target Class Distribution')
plt.xlabel('Classes')
plt.ylabel('Frequency')
plt.show()
```

Exploratory Data Analysis (EDA) is a critical first step in the machine learning pipeline, providing invaluable insights that guide model development and ensure robust performance. By using Scikit-Learn alongside Pandas, Matplotlib, and Seaborn, you can perform thorough statistical analysis, data visualization, and feature engineering, preparing your dataset for successful machine learning. EDA not only improves your understanding of the data but also helps you make informed decisions that lead to more accurate and interpretable models.

Chapter 31

Using Scikit-Learn for Quantitative Finance

Quantitative finance involves the application of mathematical models and computational techniques to financial markets, and machine learning has become a crucial tool in this domain. By leveraging historical financial data, machine learning models can assist in tasks such as **algorithmic trading**, **risk assessment**, and **portfolio optimization**. Scikit-Learn, with its rich set of tools for data preprocessing, model building, and evaluation, is well-suited for building machine learning models to address quantitative finance challenges.

In this chapter, we'll explore the role of machine learning in quantitative finance, focusing on how Scikit-Learn can be applied to various financial tasks, including price prediction, volatility forecasting, and portfolio management.

Machine Learning in Quantitative Finance: An Overview

Machine learning is revolutionizing the way quantitative analysts approach financial markets. Traditionally, quantitative finance relied on statistical models and assumptions about market behavior. However, with the advent of machine learning, more adaptive and data-driven methods are being used to make predictions and optimize investment strategies. Machine learning models can uncover patterns in financial data, model complex relationships, and make predictions based on historical data.

Key applications of machine learning in finance include:

1. **Algorithmic Trading**: Automated trading strategies that rely on machine learning to make real-time trading decisions based on patterns in market data.
2. **Risk Management**: Identifying and assessing risks in financial portfolios, including credit risk, market risk, and operational risk.
3. **Portfolio Optimization**: Optimizing asset allocation strategies using machine learning to maximize returns while minimizing risk.
4. **Price Prediction**: Using models to forecast future asset prices, such as stock prices, exchange rates, or commodity prices.

Loading Financial Data for Machine Learning

Before building machine learning models, the first step is acquiring and preparing financial data. Financial data is often time-series in nature, and many sources, such as Yahoo Finance, Alpha Vantage, or Quandl, provide historical data on asset prices, market indices, and other financial indicators.

For demonstration purposes, let's load stock price data using the **yfinance** library, which provides a convenient interface to download historical financial data from Yahoo Finance.

```
import yfinance as yf
import pandas as pd

# Download historical stock price data for a company
(e.g., Apple)
data = yf.download('AAPL', start='2020-01-01',
end='2023-01-01')

# Display the first few rows
print(data.head())
```

The dataset includes the stock's **Open**, **High**, **Low**, **Close**, **Volume**, and **Adjusted Close** prices, which are typically used as features in machine learning models.

Preprocessing Financial Data

Preprocessing financial data is essential for ensuring that machine learning models can learn meaningful patterns from the data. Common preprocessing steps in quantitative finance include:

1. **Feature Engineering**: Creating new features from raw financial data, such as **moving averages**, **momentum indicators**, and **volatility**.

2. **Handling Missing Data**: Financial data can sometimes contain gaps due to market closures or other factors. Imputation methods can be used to fill in missing values.
3. **Scaling Data**: Many machine learning models require features to be on the same scale. In finance, it's common to scale features using **standardization** or **min-max scaling**.

Feature Engineering in Finance

Feature engineering is a critical aspect of building machine learning models in finance. By creating new features from historical price data, we can help models learn important trends and patterns in the market. Some common technical indicators used as features include:

- **Moving Average (MA)**: The average price over a given period, used to smooth out short-term fluctuations.
- **Relative Strength Index (RSI)**: A momentum indicator that measures the speed and change of price movements, used to identify overbought or oversold conditions.
- **Bollinger Bands**: A volatility indicator that consists of a moving average and two standard deviation bands.

```python
# Calculate the 20-day moving average
data['MA_20']                                =
data['Close'].rolling(window=20).mean()
```

```python
# Calculate the Relative Strength Index (RSI)
delta = data['Close'].diff(1)
gain = (delta.where(delta > 0, 0)).rolling(window=14).mean()
loss = (-delta.where(delta < 0, 0)).rolling(window=14).mean()
rs = gain / loss
data['RSI'] = 100 - (100 / (1 + rs))

print(data[['MA_20', 'RSI']].head())
```

These engineered features can provide additional predictive power to machine learning models.

Algorithmic Trading with Scikit-Learn

Algorithmic trading involves using machine learning models to make real-time decisions on when to buy or sell assets. One common approach is to use machine learning classifiers, such as **logistic regression** or **random forests**, to predict whether an asset's price will rise or fall in the next time step.

Let's build a simple algorithmic trading model using Scikit-Learn's **Logistic Regression** to predict stock price movements based on technical indicators.

```python
from sklearn.model_selection import train_test_split
from sklearn.linear_model import LogisticRegression
```

```python
from sklearn.metrics import accuracy_score

# Create target variable (1 if the next day's close price is
higher, 0 otherwise)
data['Target']      =      (data['Close'].shift(-1)      >
data['Close']).astype(int)

# Select features and target
X = data[['MA_20', 'RSI']].dropna()
y = data['Target'].dropna()

# Split the data into training and testing sets
X_train, X_test, y_train, y_test = train_test_split(X, y,
test_size=0.3, random_state=42)

# Train a logistic regression model
model = LogisticRegression()
model.fit(X_train, y_train)

# Make predictions on the test set
y_pred = model.predict(X_test)

# Evaluate the model's accuracy
accuracy = accuracy_score(y_test, y_pred)
print(f'Model Accuracy: {accuracy:.2f}')
```

This simple model uses the moving average and RSI to predict whether the stock's price will rise the next day. More complex models can incorporate additional features and utilize more advanced algorithms such as **XGBoost**, **random forests**, or **deep learning** for higher accuracy.

Risk Assessment Using Scikit-Learn

Risk assessment is another important area in quantitative finance. Machine learning can help assess various types of financial risks, including:

- **Credit Risk**: Predicting the likelihood that a borrower will default on a loan.
- **Market Risk**: Assessing the potential losses due to market movements.
- **Operational Risk**: Evaluating risks associated with business operations.

One popular application of machine learning in credit risk is building classification models to predict defaults. Scikit-Learn provides several classification algorithms, such as **decision trees**, **random forests**, and **support vector machines (SVM)**, which can be applied to credit risk data.

```
from sklearn.ensemble import RandomForestClassifier

# Assume 'X_credit' and 'y_credit' are features and
target for credit risk dataset
# Train a random forest model for credit risk prediction
rf_model = RandomForestClassifier()
```

```
rf_model.fit(X_credit_train, y_credit_train)

# Predict and evaluate
y_credit_pred = rf_model.predict(X_credit_test)
credit_accuracy    =    accuracy_score(y_credit_test,
y_credit_pred)
print(f'Credit      Risk      Model      Accuracy:
{credit_accuracy:.2f}')
```

Portfolio Optimization with Machine Learning

Portfolio optimization aims to balance returns and risks by selecting the optimal combination of assets. Traditional optimization methods rely on **Modern Portfolio Theory (MPT)** and the **Markowitz efficient frontier**, but machine learning offers a data-driven approach to finding the best asset allocation.

One way to optimize portfolios with machine learning is to predict the future returns of assets and use these predictions to guide the allocation strategy. By combining machine learning models with optimization algorithms, such as **quadratic programming** or **genetic algorithms**, you can maximize portfolio returns while managing risk.

```
from sklearn.linear_model import LinearRegression

# Train a model to predict future returns of assets
X_portfolio = historical_returns_features
```

```
y_portfolio = future_returns
reg_model = LinearRegression()
reg_model.fit(X_portfolio_train, y_portfolio_train)

# Use the model's predictions to inform portfolio
allocation
predicted_returns                              =
reg_model.predict(X_portfolio_test)
```

In this example, a **linear regression** model is used to predict future returns based on historical returns and other market indicators. The predicted returns can then be fed into an optimization algorithm to find the optimal asset allocation.

Challenges in Quantitative Finance

Quantitative finance poses several unique challenges when applying machine learning, including:

1. **Non-stationarity**: Financial data is often non-stationary, meaning that statistical properties like mean and variance can change over time. This makes it difficult for machine learning models to generalize across different market conditions.
2. **Noisy Data**: Financial data is notoriously noisy, and many short-term price movements are random or influenced by external factors that cannot be predicted by models.

3. **Overfitting**: Given the noise and complexity of financial markets, there is a high risk of overfitting, where models perform well on historical data but fail to generalize to future market conditions.
4. **Data Availability**: In some areas of finance, such as high-frequency trading, access to large amounts of high-quality data is crucial for building accurate models. However, acquiring such data can be expensive and time-consuming.

Machine learning is becoming an indispensable tool in quantitative finance, helping analysts and traders automate trading strategies, assess risks, and optimize portfolios.

Chapter 32

Automating Machine Learning with Scikit-Learn and AutoML

Machine learning has increasingly become an integral part of data-driven decision-making, but developing effective models involves several complex steps, including model selection, hyperparameter tuning, and deployment. To streamline these processes and make machine learning more accessible, AutoML (Automated Machine Learning) tools have emerged. These tools automate many of the tasks associated with building machine learning models, enabling practitioners to focus on problem-solving rather than the intricacies of model development.

In this chapter, we will explore the concept of AutoML, how it integrates with Scikit-Learn, and the benefits and limitations of automating the machine learning workflow.

Introduction to AutoML

AutoML refers to a set of techniques and tools designed to automate the machine learning pipeline. This includes:

- **Model Selection**: Choosing the best model from a range of algorithms.

- **Hyperparameter Tuning**: Optimizing the parameters of models to enhance performance.
- **Feature Engineering**: Automatically generating and selecting features that improve model accuracy.
- **Model Deployment**: Streamlining the process of deploying models into production environments.

The goal of AutoML is to democratize machine learning by making it easier for non-experts to build effective models and allowing experts to focus on more strategic aspects of their work.

Scikit-Learn's Role in AutoML

Scikit-Learn is a powerful library for machine learning in Python, providing tools for model building, evaluation, and preprocessing. While Scikit-Learn does not include AutoML features directly, it can be integrated with various AutoML frameworks that leverage its capabilities.

AutoML Frameworks Compatible with Scikit-Learn

Several AutoML frameworks are compatible with Scikit-Learn and can be used to automate different parts of the machine learning pipeline:

1. **TPOT (Tree-based Pipeline Optimization Tool)**: TPOT uses genetic algorithms to optimize machine learning pipelines. It can automatically select the best

preprocessing steps and models, and tune hyperparameters.

2. **Auto-sklearn**: This framework extends Scikit-Learn by adding automatic model selection and hyperparameter optimization capabilities. It uses meta-learning and ensemble techniques to improve model performance.

3. **H2O.ai**: H2O.ai provides AutoML functionality through its H2O library, which integrates with Scikit-Learn and offers automated machine learning workflows, including model training and hyperparameter tuning.

4. **Google AutoML**: Google's AutoML tools can be used in conjunction with Scikit-Learn for advanced automated model development. Although primarily hosted on Google Cloud, it offers integration points for various data science tools.

Using TPOT for AutoML

TPOT is an open-source Python library that automates the process of machine learning pipeline optimization. It uses evolutionary algorithms to search through different combinations of preprocessing steps and machine learning models to find the best-performing pipeline.

Here's a basic example of how to use TPOT with Scikit-Learn:

```python
from tpot import TPOTClassifier
from sklearn.datasets import load_iris
from sklearn.model_selection import train_test_split
from sklearn.metrics import accuracy_score

# Load dataset
data = load_iris()
X = data.data
y = data.target

# Split dataset
X_train, X_test, y_train, y_test = train_test_split(X, y,
test_size=0.3, random_state=42)

# Initialize and train TPOT model
tpot = TPOTClassifier(verbosity=2, generations=5,
population_size=20, random_state=42)
tpot.fit(X_train, y_train)

# Make predictions and evaluate
y_pred = tpot.predict(X_test)
accuracy = accuracy_score(y_test, y_pred)
print(f'TPOT Model Accuracy: {accuracy:.2f}')

# Export the best pipeline
tpot.export('best_model_pipeline.py')
```

In this example, TPOT automatically explores different model and preprocessing combinations to find the best pipeline for the Iris dataset. The final pipeline can be exported for further use or deployment.

Using Auto-sklearn

Auto-sklearn is another popular AutoML tool that extends Scikit-Learn. It performs automated model selection and hyperparameter tuning by leveraging meta-learning and ensemble methods.

Here's a simple example of using Auto-sklearn with Scikit-Learn:

```
import autosklearn.classification
from sklearn.datasets import load_iris
from sklearn.model_selection import train_test_split
from sklearn.metrics import accuracy_score

# Load dataset
data = load_iris()
X = data.data
y = data.target

# Split dataset
X_train, X_test, y_train, y_test = train_test_split(X, y,
test_size=0.3, random_state=42)

# Initialize and train Auto-sklearn model
automl                                              =
autosklearn.classification.AutoSklearnClassifier(time_
```

```
left_for_this_task=120,          per_run_time_limit=30,
seed=42)
automl.fit(X_train, y_train)

# Make predictions and evaluate
y_pred = automl.predict(X_test)
accuracy = accuracy_score(y_test, y_pred)
print(f'Auto-sklearn Model Accuracy: {accuracy:.2f}')
```

In this example, Auto-sklearn automates the process of model selection and hyperparameter tuning for the Iris dataset. The time_left_for_this_task parameter specifies how long Auto-sklearn should search for the optimal model.

Integrating AutoML with Scikit-Learn Pipelines

AutoML frameworks often rely on Scikit-Learn's pipeline infrastructure to build and optimize models. Scikit-Learn pipelines streamline the process of chaining together preprocessing steps and model training. AutoML tools can use these pipelines to systematically explore different combinations of preprocessing and modeling steps.

For example, you can integrate TPOT or Auto-sklearn with a custom Scikit-Learn pipeline to include specific preprocessing steps or feature engineering techniques.

```
from sklearn.pipeline import Pipeline
```

```python
from sklearn.preprocessing import StandardScaler
from sklearn.decomposition import PCA
from tpot import TPOTClassifier

# Define a pipeline with preprocessing steps
pipeline = Pipeline([
    ('scaler', StandardScaler()),
    ('pca', PCA(n_components=2)),
    ('classifier',              TPOTClassifier(verbosity=2,
generations=5, population_size=20, random_state=42))
])

# Load dataset and split
data = load_iris()
X = data.data
y = data.target
X_train, X_test, y_train, y_test = train_test_split(X, y,
test_size=0.3, random_state=42)

# Train the pipeline
pipeline.fit(X_train, y_train)

# Make predictions and evaluate
y_pred = pipeline.predict(X_test)
accuracy = accuracy_score(y_test, y_pred)
print(f'Pipeline Accuracy: {accuracy:.2f}')
```

This example demonstrates how to use a Scikit-Learn pipeline with TPOT to include preprocessing steps such as scaling and PCA before model training.

Benefits of AutoML

1. **Efficiency**: AutoML automates repetitive tasks, saving time and allowing data scientists to focus on more strategic aspects of their work.
2. **Accessibility**: It lowers the barrier to entry for individuals without extensive machine learning expertise by simplifying the model-building process.
3. **Optimization**: AutoML tools systematically explore and tune models, often resulting in better performance compared to manual tuning.
4. **Consistency**: Automated processes reduce the variability that can occur with manual model selection and hyperparameter tuning.

Limitations of AutoML

1. **Computational Cost**: AutoML can be computationally expensive, particularly with large datasets and complex models.
2. **Lack of Customization**: Automated processes may not always produce the most tailored models for specific use cases or data characteristics.
3. **Overfitting Risk**: As with any automated tool, there is a risk of overfitting if the search space is not

adequately constrained or if the tool is not used correctly.

4. **Transparency**: Automated models may lack transparency, making it challenging to understand the rationale behind certain decisions or configurations.

AutoML tools offer powerful capabilities for automating the machine learning pipeline, from model selection and hyperparameter tuning to deployment. By integrating AutoML frameworks with Scikit-Learn, data scientists and machine learning practitioners can streamline the model-building process and focus on higher-level aspects of their work. While AutoML brings many benefits, including efficiency and accessibility, it also has limitations that should be considered. Understanding how to effectively use AutoML and Scikit-Learn together can greatly enhance the ability to build robust and effective machine learning models.

Chapter 33

Future Directions in Machine Learning with Scikit-Learn

As machine learning continues to evolve rapidly, staying informed about emerging trends and advancements is crucial for practitioners looking to leverage the latest techniques and tools. Scikit-Learn, as a prominent library in the Python ecosystem, is continuously updated to address new challenges and incorporate advancements in the field. In this final chapter, we will explore the future directions of machine learning, emerging trends, and how Scikit-Learn is evolving to meet these new demands. We will also discuss next steps for mastering advanced machine learning applications.

Emerging Trends in Machine Learning

The landscape of machine learning is shifting with several key trends shaping the future of the field. These trends include advancements in model architectures, increased focus on explainability and fairness, and the integration of machine learning with other domains such as healthcare and finance.

1. Advanced Model Architectures

Machine learning models are becoming more sophisticated, with advancements in model architectures driving new capabilities and applications. Some notable developments include:

- **Transformers and Attention Mechanisms**: Originally developed for natural language processing, transformers and attention mechanisms are now being applied to a wide range of tasks, including computer vision and time series forecasting. These architectures enable models to handle long-range dependencies and complex relationships in data.
- **Generative Models**: Models such as Generative Adversarial Networks (GANs) and Variational Autoencoders (VAEs) are gaining popularity for their ability to generate synthetic data, perform data augmentation, and create realistic samples in various domains.
- **Graph Neural Networks (GNNs)**: GNNs are designed to work with data represented as graphs, making them particularly useful for applications involving social networks, molecular structures, and recommendation systems.

2. Explainability and Fairness

As machine learning models are increasingly used in critical applications, the need for explainability and fairness is becoming more pronounced. Key areas of focus include:

- **Model Interpretability**: Tools and techniques for interpreting machine learning models are evolving to provide more transparency into model decisions. Techniques such as SHAP (SHapley Additive exPlanations) and LIME (Local Interpretable Model-agnostic Explanations) are helping practitioners understand and trust their models.
- **Bias and Fairness**: Addressing bias and ensuring fairness in machine learning models is a growing concern. Researchers and practitioners are developing methods to detect and mitigate bias in data and model predictions, aiming to create more equitable outcomes.

3. Integration with Other Domains

Machine learning is increasingly being integrated with other fields to address complex real-world problems. Notable integrations include:

- **Healthcare**: Machine learning is being used to advance personalized medicine, improve diagnostic accuracy, and accelerate drug discovery. Integration with electronic health records and medical imaging is driving innovations in healthcare.
- **Finance**: In finance, machine learning is enhancing algorithmic trading, fraud detection, and risk assessment. The integration of machine learning with financial data is enabling more sophisticated analysis and decision-making.

- **IoT and Edge Computing**: The rise of Internet of Things (IoT) devices and edge computing is driving the need for machine learning models that can operate in resource-constrained environments and make real-time decisions.

Scikit-Learn's Evolution

Scikit-Learn continues to evolve to keep pace with these emerging trends and meet new challenges in machine learning. The library's development focuses on enhancing existing functionalities, incorporating new algorithms, and improving usability. Some areas of evolution include:

1. Enhanced Model Support

Scikit-Learn is regularly updated to include new machine learning algorithms and techniques. Recent additions include:

- **Support for New Algorithms**: Scikit-Learn has incorporated advanced algorithms, such as Gradient Boosting Machines (GBMs) and ensemble methods, to improve model performance and flexibility.
- **Integration with Other Libraries**: Scikit-Learn is increasingly integrating with other Python libraries, such as TensorFlow and PyTorch, to support hybrid approaches that leverage deep learning and traditional machine learning techniques.

2. Improved Usability and Documentation

Scikit-Learn developers are focused on enhancing the library's usability and documentation to make it more accessible and easier to use:

- **User-Friendly APIs**: Efforts are being made to simplify APIs and improve the consistency of function signatures, making it easier for users to apply machine learning techniques.
- **Comprehensive Documentation**: The library's documentation is continuously updated with detailed explanations, examples, and tutorials to help users understand and apply Scikit-Learn's features effectively.

3. Scalability and Performance

Scikit-Learn is also working on improving scalability and performance to handle larger datasets and more complex models:

- **Efficient Computation**: Optimizations are being made to enhance the efficiency of algorithms and reduce computational overhead, enabling faster training and evaluation.
- **Integration with Distributed Computing**: Efforts are underway to integrate Scikit-Learn with distributed computing frameworks, such as Dask, to manage large-scale data and accelerate model training.

Next Steps in Mastering Advanced Machine Learning Applications

To stay at the forefront of machine learning and fully leverage the capabilities of Scikit-Learn, consider the following next steps:

1. Explore Advanced Topics

Dive deeper into advanced topics such as deep learning, reinforcement learning, and unsupervised learning. Explore how these areas intersect with traditional machine learning and how they can be applied to solve complex problems.

2. Stay Updated with Research

Keep up with the latest research and advancements in machine learning by reading academic papers, attending conferences, and participating in online forums. Staying informed about cutting-edge techniques will help you apply the latest methods to your projects.

3. Contribute to the Community

Contribute to the machine learning community by sharing your knowledge, collaborating on open-source projects, and participating in discussions. Engaging with the community can provide valuable insights and help you stay connected with developments in the field.

4. Build Real-World Projects

Apply your skills to real-world projects and case studies to gain practical experience. Building and deploying machine learning models in real-world scenarios will deepen your understanding and improve your ability to tackle diverse challenges.

5. Continuously Learn and Adapt

Machine learning is a dynamic field with rapid advancements. Embrace a mindset of continuous learning and adaptation to stay relevant and effectively address new challenges as they arise.

The future of machine learning is characterized by rapid advancements, emerging trends, and evolving challenges. Scikit-Learn, as a key tool in the machine learning ecosystem, continues to adapt and expand to meet these new demands. By staying informed about emerging trends, leveraging Scikit-Learn's evolving capabilities, and pursuing advanced learning opportunities, practitioners can master the art of machine learning and drive innovation in their fields. As the landscape of machine learning continues to evolve, embracing these changes and continuously developing your skills will be essential for achieving success in this exciting and ever-changing field.

www.ingramcontent.com/pod-product-compliance
Lightning Source LLC
LaVergne TN
LVHW051431050326
832903LV00030BD/3025